# Sweet Tales from the Bitter Edge

# Sweet Tales from the Bitter Edge

## Chasing God with Jacob's limp

**Gethin Russell-Jones**

Scripture Union

Scripture Union, 207–209 Queensway, Bletchley, MK2 2EB, England.

Email: info@scriptureunion.org.uk
Internet: http://www.scriptureunion.org.uk

© Copyright Gethin Russell-Jones 2000

First published 2000
ISBN 1 85999 297 8

Scripture taken from: The HOLY BIBLE, NEW INTERNATIONAL VERSION. Copyright © 1973, 1978, 1984 by International Bible Society. Anglicisation copyright © 1979, 1984, 1989. Used by permission of Hodder and Stoughton Limited. *The Contemporary English Version*, ©1997 British and Foreign Bible Society. *The Message*. Copyright © by Eugene H Peterson, 1993, 1994, 1995. Used by permission of NavPress Publishing Group.

The poem by Jack Clemo (page 42) is used with permission. It is published in the *New Oxford Book of Christian Verse*, ed Donald Davie, Oxford University Press, 1981. The four lines by Dylan Thomas (page 60) are taken from 'And death shall have no dominion', first published in *25 Poems* (1936).

British Library Cataloguing-in-Publication Data
A catalogue record for this book is available from the British Library.

Cover design by ie Design.
Cover photograph by Janey Napier.
Printed and bound in Great Britain by Stanley L Hunt (Printers) Ltd, Rushden, Northamptonshire.

*To Clare, my sweetest tale.*

# Contents

## About Gethin Russell-Jones, author of *Sweet Tales from the Bitter Edge*

Gethin's career has not always been poetic. He describes working in a pasta restaurant as 'the hardest work I've ever done.' Somewhere along the road, he has trained as a barrister, sold telesales ads and worked on a radio station. But foundational to his writing is the time he spent pastoring two Baptist churches, which has drawn out of him an impulse to describe in words the gracious activity of God in the lives of broken people.

'Life is complicated and often messy,' says Gethin. 'People make decisions because of all kinds of complex motivations, and we don't always choose wisely. But God is there in the midst of us and, amazingly, is concerned about our disasters and tragedies, and our ordinariness. Sometimes he is silent, sometimes he is surprising. Sometimes he turns a situation around overnight. But, more often, he wrestles with us or gently nudges us through slow erratic healing to life.'

Yes, Gethin was born in Wales. And, yes, he really does now live in Milton Keynes, working in journalism and public relations. He is married to Clare, and they have four children.

# They read it first, and they said...

'If you want a quiet life, don't touch this book. It reads like poetry, but smashes into comfortable, self-satisfied Christianity like an axe splintering wood. A great read.'
**Evangelist Rev Rob Frost**

'Trust the title of this book – Jesus tramping through the ruins of humanity. Strong stuff, but I dare you not to read it.'
**Adrian Plass**

'This book is for anyone who is tired of pretending that life's OK. Its charming honesty will leave few readers unmoved. Cutting through comfortable Christianity, it dwells with people and issues that our success culture would sooner forget. Above all, SWEET TALES FROM THE BITTER EDGE recounts true stories of the amazing grace of God, and the warmth of the welcome he gives the lonely, the lost and the least. The power of transforming love. I warmly commend this book.' **The Right Rev James Jones, Bishop of Liverpool**

'The honesty of his storytelling is great. All the stuff about addictions is great, too. What struck me is that the author actually suggests that being on the "sick roll" is inevitable and healthy ... that labelling yourself as being sick is the only way to be honest, and that the answer doesn't lie in finding balance and learning to live with compromise ... but rather in struggling continually.' **Jonathan, student psychiatric nurse**

'For believers feeling by turns blessed and beaten-up, this book provides welcome confirmation that life on the edge as a Christian may be uncomfortable, but it isn't unusual. A lyrical and painfully honest exploration of the Christian life, caught between the now and the not-yet of discipleship. For climbers at the rockface, hanging on by their fingernails.' **Russ Bravo, Editor, Christian Herald**

'The rawness of emotions in the book takes the reader on a "white-knuckle" ride through life's extremes. It is like walking along a knife-edge, seeking the adrenaline rush of falling into a black hole – or choosing to lean the other way in faith "certain of what we do not see" into Jesus' arms.' **Anne Mason, Prison Fellowship**

'These stories twin a rare blend of honesty with hope – where rawness meets reality.' **John Buckeridge, Editor, Christianity and Youthwork**

'A book for those who feel themselves on the outside looking in, who feel born in a world to which everyone has the map but them.' **Ruth Gledhill, Religion Correspondent, The Times**

'Gethin Russell-Jones captured the complete spectrum of my emotions in his sharp and poetic storytelling. So personal are these documentaries, I often felt my eyes were intruding at such raw testimonies, but compelled to read on as they radiated truth and familiarity. Hard-hitting reality laced with metaphoric beauty creates a vivid journey into the lives of those we all have something in common with.' **Stella, twenty-something mother**

'A timely reminder that biblical heroes often have feet of clay; that life for many – believers and unbelievers alike – is both puzzling and unfair; and that God, in his mysterious majesty, remains the focal point of our hopes and dreams. The author's reckless honesty about himself brings the book to a poignant and provocative conclusion.' **John Capon, Editor, Baptist Times**

'I'm sorry, I don't do pre plugs.' **Ian Hislop, Editor, Private Eye**

# intro

I'm in urban parkland, surrounded by majestic trees, take-away litter and the drone of traffic. A woman pushes her daughter on a swing. 'Higher, higher, Mummy!' she shouts. And then she says it: 'Run and push, Mummy! Run and push!'

Run and push. I want that to be the story of my life.

This book is about **running and pushing** after God. Keeping going when your scaffold is collapsing and moving on involves threading through debris, tearing yourself on the vicious serrations of failure, fear and doubt. It's for people who are chasing after God with Jacob's limp.

Excuse me?

Jacob was one of the great heroes of the Bible. Full of faith, pioneering achievements and all that. He was also a liar, a cheat and a fraud. Once, fearful of meeting his twin brother, the victim of his fraud, he came face to face with God:

Jacob was left alone, and a man wrestled with him till daybreak. When the man saw that he could not overpower him, he touched the socket of Jacob's hip so that his hip was wrenched as he wrestled with the man. Then the man said, 'Let me go, for it is daybreak.'

But Jacob replied, 'I will not let you go unless you bless me.'

The man asked him, 'What is your name?'

...because you have struggled with God and with men and have overcome.

'Jacob,' he answered.

Then the man said, 'Your name will no longer be Jacob, but Israel, because you have struggled with God and with men and have overcome.'

Jacob said, 'Please tell me your name.'

But he replied, 'Why do you ask my name?' Then he blessed him there.

So Jacob called the place Peniel [face of God], saying, 'It is because I saw God face to face, and yet my life was spared.' Genesis 32:24-30

Jacob limped for the rest of his life. Whenever family, friends, neighbours, strangers caught sight of him, they would learn the cause of his limp. It was an injury resulting from his wrestling with God.

If you are:

a seeker after Jesus
limping with life's wounds
tired of trying to conceal your
disfigurement
hoping there are others who are
also limping and running
at the same time

If you are one of those people whose lives have driven them to the edge, you might find, somehow, that God is waiting for you on the precipice. In this book you will find sweet tales from that same bitter edge.

# chapter 1: park and ride

Parks are wonderful places. Acres of choice for humanity. Built for pleasure, reflection, poetry and beauty. Multiple entry points allure the pedestrian to enter and escape. You may be chained to your office, trapped in your home, entombed in mediocrity, but the park suggests a different landscape. Willows, bamboo forests, promiscuous rhododendrons, rivers, lakes, hills, play areas. Visit any park anywhere and you'll hear the sound of children whooping and laughing, dipping on swings, colliding on slides, extravagant in water. In the same park, solitary figures sit on empty benches, silent, contemplating the future, despairing of the present. Babies strapped in buggies jostle alongside the elderly trapped in wheelchairs and Zimmers.

Life is a park. Different experiences for different ages. Sometimes you visit the same spot time after time, eager to taste vivid memories, relive nourishing encounters. But other times, you pause and then go on, never to return. Living as a Christian is much the same. Chapters of faith opening at certain periods of experience. But note this. The most painful, raw, limp-ridden episodes are often the times of **greatest growth**. Bittersweet faith.

Some of my key moments happened in parks. Chatting gregariously to other eight-year-olds in Llanelli's Parc Howard, dancing fully clothed in the blue-painted paddling pool. Teenage years in Cardiff, deliberately walking into a Victorian rose garden, clutching a packet of **Gallois**. Near the folly, fingering this symbol of rebellion, striking several matches, anxiously keeping watch for parents, park keepers, teachers and any other authority figures. Gulping and gasping the nicotine, eyes watery, wondering whether I'd ever breathe again.

Then memories of long summer evenings, grazing around Roath Park in Cardiff with other adolescent boys. Football, smoking, aimlessly following groups of like-aged girls hardly aware of our amorous presence. Drab November afternoons, pockets crammed with bangers for hurling near Parkie's shed. Then there was Morgan Jones Park in Caerphilly, witness to afternoons of late pubescence and questions of faith and existence. Endless circuits of football fields and cricket pitches, picking at eternity.

Many park-less years later and I'm on Streatham Common, one of London's many lungs. I've walked to the rookery and I'm on my way down the hill, staring at the metropolis's shimmering and hazy forms. I'm hungover, spiritually desolate, lacking in direction. Kites are flying, children shouting, cars humming — and **I hear the voice of God**. Not a clap of thunder or a tearing of the heavens. More a clear apprehension. No, too tame. A direct sense that the words which filled my mind for a few seconds were not authored by me.

'Is this what you amount to? Is this what you've become? Do you like what you see?'

Slow motion impact. It took a few minutes for the import to strike, but it took my breath away. Shaken by truth, it proved to be a turning point in my walk with God.

Is this what you amount to? Is this what you've become? Do you like what you see?

Parks have:

   mazes
      slides
         roundabouts
           swings

d i t c h e s
r u b b i s h
g a n g s
c l o u d s

...pleasure, peace, noise, danger. It's the stuff of life. Life is a park, congested with changing seasons, strange encounters, moments of tranquillity. So is living under the name of Christ. It calls for movement, choices, growth, risk.

I'm in another park now. At the entrance, Edwardian trees offer a dated welcome, with shadows instead of white glare, opening beyond into a vast meadow choked with grass and weeds. Surrounding the meadow is an unbroken border of enormous trees. Not planned trees. Not the kind of trees that have been planted to hide some terrible disfigurement in the soil. Real trees. Trees that sing. Trees that move slowly and majestically. Leaves tinged and mottled with browns and reds. Planted when Victoria ruled the waves and Albert built his hall. When trams clattered, smoke belched and tuberculosis plagued the dense streets. Trees with history. Trees with attitude. Cleaning the air but holding the memory of a different history.

Reminds me of the sunglasses I bought a few years ago. First time I put them on the whole world turned to brown-green. A sepia **Dad's Army** Second-World-War kind of world. A world I don't know but find rather comforting.

Birdsong crowds the high sky. So many clouds tumbling, scudding in the ether. I carry on walking round and round the meadow. Young families eat their picnics, old men drowse on park benches. A couple of young women snigger at rude jokes behind a barricade of hands.

Another path meanders through yet more ancient trees. Now I'm in a graveyard. Not a modern, sanitised cemetery. No, there's dead life here. This place is alive with the sound of old stories. Faded lives. A criss-cross of paths, plots, mown grass and a chapel that's boarded up. This too I love. I walk on. Under a covering of leafy boughs I see the swings. 'Run and push, Mummy! Run and push!' That's what it's all about. I could stay here for ever. But I can't. There's a run-and-push life waiting to be attacked, and **ambitions** in God. And there's danger. Sweet but bitter.

This book is for people who need to limp and chase but also want to hide. For people who find the side-show more interesting than the main event. Who prefer the fringe to the festival. This book is for you:

- if you are running and pushing after God but find yourself entangled in toxic waste.

- if your light walk has become a dance of lead.

- if, to borrow the words of Henry Scougal (an eighteenth-century limp-and-chase expert), you believe in the life of God in the soul of man.

- if your deepest longing is for faith, hope and love.

- if the millennium makes you snort but the real birthday produces a song.

It's for you if you are anything like me.

# chapter 2: faith parks

I'm in a Bible theme park. Hebrews World, Gate 12. It's a word-world for people who are struggling with Christianity. People who know God and are all too aware of their own shortcomings. Frightened they won't make it. Emotions and instincts pulled by the past. Easier, happier, less hassle in the blue hills, in the rose-tinted country. Jesus may be the same yesterday, today and tomorrow, but I know my past. What's more, it becomes more and more pleasant as each day passes.

Gate 12 is especially for those who feel like losers. Losers like Jacob, who lied, cheated and moaned most of his way through life. As a young man he was cheat and a liar. As an older man he moaned, imagining that he was going to die a lot sooner than he actually did. But Jacob was loved by God.

Therefore, since we are surrounded by such a great cloud of witnesses, let us throw off everything that hinders and the sin that so easily entangles, and let us run with perseverance the race marked out for us. Let us fix our eyes on Jesus, the author and perfecter of our faith, who for the joy set before him endured the cross, scorning its shame, and sat down at the right hand of the throne of God. Consider him who endured such opposition from sinful men, so that you will not grow weary and lose heart. <u>Hebrews 12:1-3</u>

The past is a foreign country: they do things differently there.
<u>L P Hartley</u>

For what I do is not the good I want to do; no, the evil I do not want to do – this I keep on doing.

Hebrews World is all about encumbrances, entanglements and fatal attractions. A life-long chase after the most enigmatic man who ever lived. A marathon in which you sweat but which sometimes seems effortless and sweet. It's about plods and pain barriers, and being **shouted home** by a raucous rabble of saints and holy villains. Living with your head in the clouds and finding it to be home. Finding that only the heavenly-minded are of any earthly use. It's about being invaded by powers of the world to come. It's about you. It's about him.

Meet some **unlikely stars**. In the pages of this book you will meet many different people, all of them real, although I have changed their names. Their stories resound with the noises of struggle, addiction, pain and hope. These are bloodied saints.

But there are others whose names are their own. Familiar names, famous for their faith, whose stories are told in the Bible. They are included because they too have been shredded. God's love has intoxicated them, impelling them to live in his presence. At the same time, familiar poisons have mixed in with their faith. Here are people who have wrestled with God and with themselves. Strangely enough, these are the stars of Christianity. **Scarred stars**. When I look at them, I see complex people whose motives are as muddied and compromised as mine and everyone else's. Which is a problem. Modern Christianity prefers its heroes to be sin virgins. Happy, triumphant, strong. If they have 'a past', then let it remain there, a distant and forgotten event. *It was there by faith I received my sight and now I'm happy all the day*, as an old hymn puts it. This is not the Bible's version of Christian living.

> For what I do is not the good I want to do; no, the evil I do not want to do — this I keep on doing. **Romans 7:19**

Leonardo da Vinci's *Last Supper* is generally regarded as his greatest painting. It took some twenty years to complete. The people gathered round the famous table are based on real-life individuals. The story goes that one evening the artist walked the streets of Florence, searching for someone to model Jesus. He found a handsome young man, his features bathed in the mellow light of late evening. He took him back to the studio and painted him.

Twenty years later and this work of art was still incomplete. Leonardo had finished the astonishing angles and perspectives, and had painted twelve characters. All but Judas. So, after two decades, he walked the streets of Florence, again looking for a suitable face. The other portraits had been relatively straightforward, but Judas needed to have the distinctive look of a haunted man. At last he found him: flushed, angry expression, sunken eyes, his face scrawled with tension and anxiety. Poorly clothed, socially isolated. Here was Leonardo's model. Offering him financial reward, the artist invited him back to his studio to sit for the portrait.

During the sitting, a stuttering conversation developed between the two men. Yes, Leonardo had begun this painting twenty years ago and, yes, this man was a native of Florence. Surely they had met before, said 'Judas'. No, Leonardo would have remembered — he never forgot faces. Then **the terrifying fact** was revealed. As he painted the man's eyes and facial features, Leonardo sensed that he *did* know him. But where? The florin dropped. This man was once Jesus, the centrepiece of *The Last Supper*, painted over two decades before. The swing of the pendulum had brought hard times, reducing a once-handsome man to the level of a vagrant.

It's possible, indeed likely, that you are both:

a saint
    and a sinner
        at the same time

Christ was born in a stable, and he dwells today in the muck of his followers' lives. There are times of:

faith
    growth
        holiness

But there is an abundance of:

    doubts
    witherings
rebellion

You don't want to hang around Gate 12 for too long. Like as not you've already tripped up once too often and you're tangled up in sin. Fixing your eyes on Jesus sounds like sound advice, but it's not exactly practical. How do you log on and move on?

Clouds. It's all about clouds. You are surrounded by a cloud of witnesses and, if you take a little time to look at them, you'll get a new angle on God and you.

The cloud of witnesses is given its airing in Hebrews World, Gate 11. It's a list of people whom God blessed because they had faith. Even when everything seemed hopeless, they trusted God more than their circumstances. But get this. Most of them were also liars, adulterers, prostitutes, addicts, murderers.

Here's how it starts:

Now faith is being sure of what we hope for and certain of what we do not see. This is what the ancients were commended for.

...they trusted God more than their circumstances.

By faith we understand that the universe was formed at God's command, so that what is seen was not made out of what was visible.
Hebrews 11:1-3

People who believed God more than their circumstances. Often dire circumstances. Who believed that God's promises to them were more powerful than their difficulties, backgrounds, failings. Who followed their understanding of God's word, having to deal with their own mess at the same time. People like you.

So forget the fanfare. Don't bother with the red carpet. Don't call them saints if you have in mind people whose breath is always fresh, whose prayer is always powerful, who live in big houses and who, of course, give to the poor. Forget it.

These are **shop-soiled saints**, flawed by their own shortcomings. Capable of believing God for anything. Also capable of being immature, deceitful and stupid. The heroes of Hebrews World Gate 11 have rough and raw stories.

Entanglements, sweaty limping and chasing, and clouds. These speak of three spiritual appetites which start, repeat and are recycled during our faith journey. **Entanglements** are what we love to get caught in. Christians, too, like playing near the waste outlets. Sometimes they make mud pies in the sewage because they want to. Other times they feel they were put in the way of the sewage by others. The result is much the same. Guilt, condemnation, spiritual mutilation. You can't play with toxic waste without it getting right under your skin and into your soul.

Simply being an adult is hard enough. No one prepares you for it. No degrees or NVQs. One person's entanglement is another's cry of liberation. Many experience both at the same time. We used to call it sin. Nothing wrong with that as far as three-letter words go. Except no one really understands what it

Mr Lely, I desire you would use all your skill to paint my picture truly like me, and not flatter me at all; but remark all these roughnesses, pimples, warts, and everything as you see me, otherwise I will never pay a farthing for it.
Oliver Cromwell

means any more. Naughty sex and lying?

Another word is addiction. This has acquired designer status in counselling-speak, but it hides a profound meaning. An addict is someone who needs poison. The very thing he craves is the very thing that will kill him. The addict is a paradox. He's **choosing death**, mistaking it for life. Another kick. Another hit.

We are all addicts. Some are more addicted than others. We are addicted to:

alcohol
   drugs
      twisted sex

(Well, of course we are. Thank God for that. Thought there were a few nastier ones than that lurking in the Bible pile.)

But there are others. More subtle. More painful.

Maybe you reach 30 and realise that you're on your own. Decisions have to be made, responsibilities shouldered. So although you feel like you are in short trousers, with all the maturity of a second-hand romper suit, you are wrong. You are an adult. For you there is the world — **the oyster and the diamond**. For you too there is **the cry of the raven** in the still hours.

There are:

money problems
   fears
     guilt
       memories
      food

I'm going to give you a quote. I want you to hear it now. The first time I heard it, I was sitting in a church meeting, licking some old wounds, salivating on nostalgia, regret and self-pity. The preacher was African. The church was in England.

I was in the land of my origin. He was displaced, removed. But — and here's the difference — I was crouched, stationary, rehearsing my pain to any passing audience. He was running and pushing with all his might. In one sentence he told me that the greatest block to running hard after Jesus is the long memory: 'Retentive memory is a good thing. But the ability to forget is a token of greatness.'

A few more addictions to throw into the cocktail:

s e x u a l i t y

Not whether you're having it, or with whom, or how often. It's more profound than that. It's about who you are:

m a s c u l i n e ?
f e m i n i n e ?

Male and female he created them. In his image. He saw it was very good. Or very disturbing, if not laughable. Our confused, wonderful, stabbing relationships somehow represent him. Yet it's all about how innocence gets polluted. How we forge relationships with others because of our own overwhelming needs. How we lean on others because we're terrified of what's out there. Because it's sometimes about relationships which are:

b a s e d   o n   m u t u a l   i n s e c u r i t y
s a m e - s e x   h i d e a w a y s
n o n - e x i s t e n t

But Christians are not the same as other men and women. Their sins are executed before the face of Christ. Their addictions are acted out in the wake of following Jesus. They are possessed by God — but intrigued by the devil's schemes.

...possessed by God — but intrigued by the devil's schemes.

A few years ago I was hit by a bombshell:  **I am not what I seem**. Neither are most of the people I know.

Somewhere in Galatians it says that Christians can call God, 'Daddy'. Actually — and this is the thing that shook me — it doesn't say that. It says that **the Spirit within us** cries, 'Abba, Daddy!'

There is somebody else living within you. The Spirit of God is worshipping the Father. And he's doing it through you. You are occupied by another personality. You are the building, cathedral, big top, conference hall, rave, in which God is worshipping God.

Sweat. Running and pushing. Better still, limping. It's what people used to call perseverance. By which they meant 'grin and bear it'. And:

> put up and shut up
>    go to church
>      read the Bible
>        give your money
>          be nice
>            don't be naughty

Perseverance sounds like treading water, putting a lot of energy into staying afloat but without actually getting anywhere. But it's not true. A life full of limps is a very full life. Living a life that's full, expressive, committed and passionate about Jesus. Running so hard, that when the obstacles come, you get hurt and you get God. Not - to borrow an expression of Paul's - that I have made it.

Paul who?

**A life full of limps is a very full life.**

The man who wrote half of the New Testament and established hundreds of churches all over the Roman Empire. Who had also been a religious bigot and murdered his enemies. Whose words could wound, ridicule, soothe and comfort. Paul had experienced the overwhelming kindness of God and could relate it to others in words of human warmth. But even as a follower of Jesus, he still wrote off others whose views didn't conform to his.

On a few, very few, occasions I know that when the life of God is flowing in me, **giants seem like grasshoppers**.

You have said to yourself, Why?

Why do I know the book but I haven't met the author for some time?

Why are pagans always happier than me?

Why have I got no roots when I really want to belong?

There was once a man called Sisyphus. Because of his insolence towards the gods, he was condemned to the most futile and frustrating punishment. Each day he had to push a boulder to the top of a particular hill, only to see it roll down the other side. Every day. A lot of pushing but no destination. A lot of pushing but no point. That's what Christianity becomes when there's no vital connection to Jesus Christ. All limp and no chase. You can easily become:

> punch-drunk
> > war-weary
> > > charity-fatigued

Many of us end up like the Duke of York, a grand old failure. Like Sisyphus he had a thing about hills. He marched his army to the top and then to the bottom and then back up again.

There's only one known remedy. Fixing yourself to Jesus. Getting a regular fix of Jesus. Fixing ourselves to the church, the manifestation of his presence and glory.

And don't forget the clouds and the people who live in them.

They surround us, shouting us on. We are not alone. The book of Hebrews is full of unexpected shocks. It says that we have 'tasted the powers of the age to come'. Our lives are constantly being invaded by outsiders wanting to become insiders. The art of running and pushing doesn't depend on my religious abilities or skills. It depends largely on my capacity to embrace:

the life of God
the friends of God
the Son of God
the many clouds of God

We need reminding that we are not in this Christian life alone. Being alone is never God's intention for the believer. Adam was lonely in the midst of God's splendour, and God gave him someone to love and share his life with.

Sometimes the weight of God's truth and glory can make us feel lonely. We need each other. We need church. We need nourishing, replenishing relationships. We need covenant with God and fellowship with others. We need a sense of history. We've come from somewhere, but we're going **somewhere even better**.

# chapter 3: when a man loves a woman

> By faith Isaac blessed Jacob and Esau in regard to their future.
>
> By faith Jacob, when he was dying, blessed each of Joseph's sons, and worshipped as he leaned on the top of his staff. <u>Hebrews 11:20-21</u>

According to the German theologian Rudolf Otto, we sometimes enjoy **numinous** experiences. Times in which I, the creature, become aware of God as **wholly other**. Beware. These experiences happen infrequently, but when they do, prepare for sea change. Something not unlike this happened to the infamous liar and cheat, Jacob, son of Isaac. God blessed him — and his brother Esau. (I love that part of the story. Esau was cheated out of everything by his brother and it seemed as though God must be against him. Wrong. God *was* with him, even though he was going nowhere.)

While out travelling, and looking for a wife, Jacob spent a night sleeping in the open air. Although not a public park, it was a wide open space of common land. More or less. He dreamed of an epic staircase, complete with angels and the voice of God. He awoke, overwhelmed by the wholly otherness of God:

> When Jacob awoke from his sleep, he thought, 'Surely the LORD is in this place, and I was not aware of it.' He was afraid and said, 'How

awesome is this place! This is none other than the house of God; this is the gate of heaven.'

Early the next morning Jacob took the stone he had placed under his head and set it up as a pillar and poured oil on top of it. He called that place Bethel [house of God], though the city used to be called Luz. <u>Genesis 28:16-19</u>

Throughout his life, Jacob was a compulsive liar. Lied to his father, cheated his brother out of his legal inheritance, lied to his father-in-law. In fact, he lied to anyone. But God used him and honoured him. So highly did God esteem Jacob that he gave him a name that would one day identify an entire nation: *Israel*. Israel means 'to wrestle'. Jacob started out as a liar, became a wrestler — but ended his days a worshipper.

God loved Jacob for the same reason that he loves us. There is **no reason**. Other than his love. And his mercy, wild and unpredictable. It is also consistent. He had promised to bless Abraham's descendants and Jacob was one of those.

God had also promised, through that one man, to bless all the nations of the world. And Debbie is part of that sweeping benediction.

**Debbie is a man**. He is also a woman. Born in pre-Mussolini Italy, Debbie arrives like any other baby. Kicking and screaming. But there is one major difference. Debbie comes complete with a penis and vagina. Born in Milan to an Italian father and an English mother, he grows up without the security of personal gender. Olive skin, blonde hair and a slight build accentuate his sense of being different. Family photographs of the period reveal a stunning boy, not unlike the boy from Visconti's Death in Venice or George Eliot's Silas Marner.

This is a rare but real disorder and it's called *hermaphroditism*: 'a human being in which both male and female sex organs are

Sweet tale: Debbie, who was called Roberto.

present, or in which the sex organs contain both ovarian and testicular tissue' (The Oxford English Reference Dictionary, 1996). **Hermaphrodite** (*her-maf-ro-dit*): A person or animal with indeterminate sexual organs, or those of both sexes; a flower containing both male and female reproductive organs. The word, as you can discover in Brewer's Concise Dictionary of Phrase and Fable, is derived from Hermaphroditus, the son of Hermes and Aphrodite. The nymph Salmacis became enamoured of him and prayed that she might be so closely united that 'the twain might become one flesh'. Her prayer being heard, nymph and boy became one body.

For the first part of his life Debbie is called Roberto. He feels like a girl but has to behave like a boy. His parents conceal from him the horror of his condition, hoping that forced masculinity will cure him. At the age of 13, Roberto and his family move to the Midlands town of Wolverhampton, moving in with his English grandmother.

Further complications. Roberto's father is an Italian Jew. Quite a problem. Britain declares war on Germany for the second time and Italy soon sides with Herr Hitler. Roberto's father, a cash-strapped interior decorator, becomes the enemy. A potential spy. Debbie's memory of the period is hazy, disfigured by subsequent decades of torture. She insists that her father's curious status as both Semitic and Italian was viewed with alarm by the military authorities. Tried by a military court, he 'disappears'. True? Many savageries happen during that period, hidden even from the 30-year rule. On the other hand, Debbie's visceral pain may simply have composed another *danse macabre* in her mind.

For twenty years he conceals this **desperate secret**, that she is both male and female. Society has the climate of cold guilt and judgement. Illiterate in the art of forgiveness.

A combination of Aryan good looks and keen intelligence

give Roberto a surprisingly easy passage to higher education. Three years at a northern university might have given him the emotional liberation he craves. But no. He feels like a prisoner, padlocked to a strange body.

At twenty-one he leaves university and is articled to a firm of Leicester solicitors. By now he has developed as both a man and woman. His sexuality is a torment to him, and he is in constant pain. His genitalia are raw and sore. He can't urinate without extreme, crucifying agony. And then there are periods. Working in a cramped office, each executive segregated by a strict division of labour, Roberto feels lonely and uncomfortable. Yet happy to have found a trade and esteemed by his boss as a good worker.

Every month he feels as though his genitals are being shredded by barbed wire. And every month he is bullied by his torn and angry mind. From deep mental trenches, warring emotions savage his ravaged brain. Whipped by fear, lacerated by terrifying anxiety, he walks through a crowded, noisy, imaginary circus of accusation:

q u e e r
   q u e e n
     h o m o
       t a r t

Eventually, he qualifies as a solicitor and moves to the North East, working in a large practice. This he does for twenty years. People think he is gay and either want sex or mock him. Frequently both at the same time. He has a complete nervous breakdown.

At the age of 50 Roberto makes a frightening decision. He decides to become Debbie. Following a series of consultations with his GP, specialists and numerous suitability tests, he is given medical permission. As he lies insensate on the operating table, surgical skill seeks to **clarify the confusion** of his birth.

Debbie wakes to a new world — only to find that it's much the same as the old. She buys a cottage on the Northumbrian coast and dreams of anonymity. But the small town awakens to its new-for-old resident. Her neighbours begin **a hate campaign**, alleging that Debbie is a pervert and a child molester. Household waste is dumped in her garden. Late-night callers demand sex, and she is regularly assaulted as she walks through the town.

One day, shoulders stooped and coat-wrapped, she visits a café and is befriended by a young Christian who shows her kindness. They share a cigarette and he buys her a cup of tea. They talk about religion and Christianity. Despite a life of mental nooses and emotional dungeons, Debbie believes in God. She even has a latent love for Jesus. William takes her to the church she has stopped attending — and she is surprised by love.

All of which brings us to **Isaiah 56:4**:

> To the eunuchs who keep my Sabbaths
>     who choose what pleases me
>     and hold fast to my covenant —
> to them I will give within my temple and
>         its walls
>     a memorial and a name
>     better than sons and daughters;
> I will give them an everlasting name
>     that will not be cut off.

I don't know any eunuchs, though I've heard of the legendary *castrati*: male choristers with phenomenally high voices, whose testicles were surgically removed.

Eunuchs used to be more common than they are now. Not

A new world ... much the same as the old.

merely to bring the high notes to church choirs but also for governmental purposes. At various times in history, only eunuchs could aspire to high office in the civil service. With no offspring, a eunuch had no motive for murdering a ruler for his family's sake.

But in the Old Testament, eunuchs were outsiders. They couldn't even get close to God without being reminded of their physical state. Generally speaking, if a Gentile wanted to become a Jew, he would be circumcised and allowed to take some part in Jewish worship. He would be known as a God-fearer, a friend of God. Not so the eunuch. He was cut off, dismembered from God's people. Nothing much to circumcise. And even should he memorise every Levitical law and utter every known prayer, it would avail him nothing. The eunuch was a career outsider.

You may not be a eunuch, but you may well feel like **an outsider**. You look at couples, families, friends on a night out, the church. And, however much you press your face against the pane of glass, you are an outsider. It seems that everyone else is normal, confident, getting on with life. But for you there is silence, fear, a constant need to cover your tracks.

Maybe you are:

> gay
>> a transvestite
>>> trapped in the wrong body
>>> unsure of your sexuality
>>> celibate

And there's no one you can talk to.

...for you there is silence, fear, a constant need to cover your tracks.

Think eunuch. Think **Acts 8:26-40**. A castrated outsider is reading the Bible in his chariot, on his way from Jerusalem to his home in Ethiopia. He is an important treasury official. His boss is a queen. A classic eunuch. And he's desperate for God.

He's reading some verses in Isaiah about someone who will come and suffer for people and bring them into relationship with God.

A man called Philip happens to be in the desert. He tells the eunuch that Isaiah is talking about Jesus, whom he can know for himself. Then Philip baptises him in water.

Here's the point. An outsider becomes part of the family. A friend of God. Accepted as though he's as normal as everyone else. Which, of course, is true. In the presence of Jesus we're all **as normal and as bankrupt** as each other. Once we turn to him, we find that Jesus likes our company. He forgives, reassures, and empowers a different future. In his death he makes our dark distortions his own. In his resurrection he proves that God is able to bring victory out of despair. And faith takes hold of who Jesus is now so that he can make us as new as he is.

Debbie belongs to a church. She is a member. When she's able to meet with the rest of her brothers and sisters on Sundays, she often takes part in prayer, reading a Bible passage, prophesying. **She belongs and she's needed**. Her spiritual gifts are as vital in that church as those of any of the other members.

Debbie used to be Roberto. Now she's in Christ.

# chapter 4: faithfully bankrupt

By faith Noah, when warned about things not yet seen, in holy fear built an ark to save his family. By his faith he condemned the world and became heir of the righteousness that comes by faith. Hebrews 11:7

Everyone knows Noah's story. The animals went in two by two, hurrah, hurrah. Elephants and the kangaroos ... etcetera. Happy creatures, jolly animals, indoor games during the bad weather.

This same Noah, victim of the many cheesy school assembly songs, lived through a **holocaust**. God's anger fell on everyone and everything, except Noah and his makeshift zoo. He witnessed the death of his world.

When finally his boat scraped to a dry halt on top of a mountain, Noah did something spectacularly human:

Noah, a man of the soil, proceeded to plant a vineyard. When he drank some of its wine, he became drunk and lay uncovered inside his tent. Ham, the father of Canaan, saw his father's nakedness and told his two brothers outside. But Shem and Japheth took a garment and laid it across their shoulders; then they walked in backwards and covered their father's nakedness. Their faces were turned the other way so that they would not see their father's nakedness. Genesis 9:20-23

This mighty man of faith, who built an ark in 'holy fear', got drunk and slept naked, to the shame of his family. Why? Scripture doesn't relate, except that many others have done the same thing — faced with monstrous circumstances and terrifying consequences, they have tried to blot out the pain.

During the Second World War, in a concentration camp, a group of rabbis met. They were profoundly shaken, angry, disillusioned by the ordeal suffered by their people. As they spoke, they concluded that **there must be no God**. God was dead, otherwise how could he have allowed this to happen? They announced to each other that atheism was their only option. For the sake of their own integrity, they must acknowledge the death of the divine and get on with their lives. Before they disbanded, they ... prayed together.

There are men and women of righteousness in every generation. We remember Noah on account of his ark. Take away this strange vessel and you're left with an ordinary man and his family. He was a righteous man in difficult circumstances, not unlike John.

Let me tell you the story of **John and his wife, Trish**. John is an expert at a time of utter indifference. He is able to thread himself through the inner organs of mute machines, even though they fill entire rooms. It's 1982 and he's a computer buff for a large multinational. Large house, yes. Private education for his son, certainly. Also private health care for his wife, Trish, drained by the merciless squeeze of depression. Year after year.

**Sweet tale: John and Trish, who find righteousness and great difficulties.**

Trish becomes a Christian first, despite John's male insecurities. He — bright, achieving — still retains a vestige of postwar optimism. Born and nurtured in the embattled religious cultures of South Wales, he has more pressing issues to deal with. Work, family, disintegration. But, unexpectedly, he finds faith for himself. Persuaded by Trish to attend some special meetings at her adopted church, the good news of heaven crashes into his world. He confesses Jesus.

But postnatal bombs continue to shell Trish. Three children and a body and mind full of warring chemicals mean that she is hospitalised at regular intervals. Months are spent at a private hospital in Hertfordshire, her only consolation the electric volts that chase her resident monsters. She returns to the family at weekends, but menacing shadows now fill this suburban home, which are occasionally cleared by random and irrational bursts of happiness. The children grow, as do John's career fortunes. But this is a family wincing with the pain of chronic dislocation.

An invitation. John and Trish are approached by some friends to join them for a weekend at a Christian renewal centre. The Dorset house is home to a community who believe in the power of God's love. God, for them, is a person who **restores** the sharp and lacerating uselessness of broken lives. John prays a great deal in the tiny chapel, longing for an intervention he can barely articulate. Some time during their stay they are invited into the flat of one of the community members. This woman, apparently, has a remarkable gift of hospitality. She tells John that 'things happen' when people come within the orbit of this gift. Full of Celtic anticipation, John prays that this will be the encounter that changes his wife.

The time arrives, and this vulnerable couple enter a strange atmosphere. Their host is friendly, relaxed and open. There are others there, drinking coffee, eating cake and sharing their stories. John sits, speaks when spoken to, longing for a **breakthrough** moment. Maybe a prayer, a special insight from their gregarious host. Nothing. The evening passes and the guests disperse to their rooms. John's vast balloon of optimism is pricked by the merciless jab of spiritual disappointment. Except — later that night Trish says an extraordinary thing. It's her magnificat moment. 'I've been healed. I've been healed tonight. Depression has left me.'

John can't sleep, his mind whirring with preferred futures. Middle-aged and plump, he pirouettes down the spiral staircase, heading for the silent chapel.

Despite his pleasure at being in this place of prayer, John has found himself provoked, irritated and goaded over the past few days. Here is a community founded on the assumption that being a Christian means more than giving a good confession. An assertion that a believer in Jesus has rights to a Father's blessing. These are people who talk of being filled with, baptised in the Spirit. Metaphors of immersion, bathing, soaking in a God of love. And John is irritated. 'I am a Christian and I'm trying my best,' he mutters. But he knows there is more. Much more. In the quiet chapel, he prays for a fresh encounter with the God of big things.

He gets it. Sitting, standing, kneeling in the quiet hours, John experiences wave after wave of liquid love. He is overwhelmed by an aspect of God's nature previously hidden from him.

They return home. Trish healed. John alive, empowered, excited at the prospect of living out his faith. Indeed, for a while, life for the family is like a long parenthesis. Happiness between the brackets. But they are about to fall off the edge of the paragraph. A frightening chapter is about to begin.

John is unexpectedly head-hunted by another firm. His prodigious knowledge is at last recognised in the new computer age. Having endured a machiavellian boss for several years, he wins his big break and flies to the States with Trish for an extended holiday. A new job with a new employer and massive benefits await him. They cross the pond and relax with new friends.

Disaster. They return home to find that the head-hunters have failed to deliver anything. There is **no new job**.

John hasn't handed in his notice so he returns to his old firm, only to find he has been sidelined. His boss, taking advantage of his absence, has restructured the department. Yes, he still has a desk. But it's in the corridor. It all goes from worse to intolerable, resulting in John being made redundant. They are coming out of the brackets and the storyline is about to turn nasty.

With his generous redundancy payment in the bank, John has several options. He decides on the most obvious. The new dawn of the PC has yet to reach its splendour, but there is a lot of work for an expert programmer. But nothing. He applies, is interviewed, short-listed... But nothing. Undeterred, he sets up his own business, writing easy-to-understand guide books for companies investing in new software. In his first year of trading he wins an impressive award and feels that heaven, at last, is smiling on his life. Trish still declaims her healing; his business and children are doing well.

But the well dries up. In spite of his glitzy award, fewer and fewer people seek his services. Like many others, the family stray into serious debt. Mortgage repayments build up until they can no longer sustain their standard of living. In fact, so little income is coming in they can hardly sustain anything. After weeks of severe trauma, their house is sold and they move out.

They have nowhere to move to.

Their financial plight is so dire, they can't afford rented accommodation, let alone a mortgage. So a man, his wife and three children are homeless in the moneyed city of Chichester. Having poured their now meagre belongings into a transit van, this family of five spend a cramped, sleepless and exhausted night in one of the city's car parks. God has healed Trish of

...they will struggle with total financial collapse for decades...

depression and filled John with his Spirit, only to **humiliate** them in a Bedford van.

Strangely, their faith has not deserted them. Near homelessness will be a major theme of their lives and they will struggle with total financial collapse for decades to come. But they don't waver — and this, too, will be a dominating theme in their complex fugue, in spite of pity giving way to criticism as friends tell John to pull himself together and get a job. The life of the Edwards family becomes a provocation to the lawyers, bankers and stockbrokers of Chichester.

Camping in friends' caravans and houses, they slowly piece together the various fragments of normal living. John restarts his business and eventually ekes out enough to provide for the family in a small flat. Time tumbles along. Church involvement increases, children begin to leave home, business bumps along just above the breadline.

In 1992 they uproot to East Anglia, believing that God has shown them this must be their next step. A move to more elegant rented accommodation surely signals a better period.

John secures business premises in Norwich and steadily acquires enough work to keep them going. They are still there today. No. Rather, they are still in the same area today. John's business finally collapsed, but he has avoided bankruptcy. Their living accommodation has changed three times. Elegant country living gave way to a town terrace and, finally, to an annexe in a friend's country home.

Voices from the touchline express their disappointment. God has let them down. They've let themselves down. Something should have been done to avoid **such failure**. What's the point of a life which continually spins dangerously on the edge of chaos? Life, after all, is about success and achievement. God prospers his followers.

Here are two people who:

>       are so promising
>          so gifted
>             yet constantly fight homelessness
>                and financial ruin

But John and Trish are not punch-weary Christians, drained by life's cruel vagaries. They are radicals. Constant and prophetic reminders to us all that:

▪ life does not consist in what we will wear
  tomorrow.

▪ our pursuit of financial security masks deep
  anxieties and bears witness to our silent worship
  of mammon.

▪ the Son of Man, regrettably, had nowhere to lay
  his head and this, apparently, may also be true of
  his followers.

John says that God is with them. He has always been with them. He and Trish believe that God's word is more powerful and nourishing than anything else, and they live in it. At the moment John is soaking himself in the story of Joseph, son of limping Jacob, and in particular this verse:

> 'Don't be afraid! I have no right to change
> what God has decided. You tried to harm me,
> but God made it turn out for the best...'
> **Genesis 50:19-20, CEV**

And he might do well to reflect on this:

> God is subtle but he is not malicious. **Albert
> Einstein**

And this:

### 'Neither Shadow of Turning'
I could not name a single blessing
    That came to me in disguise;
The gifts I asked arrived unmasked
    Under broad day's honest skies.

God does not play a senile game
    That wraps His mercies round
With leprous sheet, a scabbed deceit:
    His good, from the start, is sound.

There is no heaven disguised as hell,
    No jail by which we're freed;
A twist that mocks is no paradox —
    It's the devil's twist indeed.

'Deliver us from evil' — why,
    If the evil has good inside?
God's war is grim — we are bruised with Him:
    His gifts never mystified.

Jack Clemo

# chapter 5: liar, liar

A longer trip now back to Hebrews Gate 11, to meet Abraham and to reflect on why he receives more space here than anyone else:

> By faith Abraham, when called to go to a place he would later receive as his inheritance, obeyed and went, even though he did not know where he was going. By faith he made his home in the promised land like a stranger in a foreign country; he lived in tents, as did Isaac and Jacob, who were heirs with him of the same promise. For he was looking forward to the city with foundations, whose architect and builder is God.
>
> By faith Abraham, even though he was past age — and Sarah herself was barren — was enabled to become a father because he considered him faithful who had made the promise. And so from this one man, and he as good as dead, came descendants as numerous as the stars in the sky and as countless as the sand on the seashore...
>
> By faith Abraham, when God tested him, offered Isaac as a sacrifice. He who had received the promises was about to sacrifice his one and only son, even though God had said to him, 'It is through Isaac that your offspring will be reckoned.' Abraham reasoned

that God could raise the dead, and figuratively speaking, he did receive Isaac back from death. Hebrews 11:8-12,17-19

More space means that Abraham must have been very important to both author and readers. And indeed he was regarded as:

the father of the Jewish nation
a man of faith
someone to be imitated

He was also a liar. **An habitual liar**. On several occasions he passed his wife off as his sister so that he wouldn't be killed by a lustful and murderous ruler. He would rather that his wife be wedded to someone else than take the consequences of them appearing together as man and wife.

Now there was a famine in the land, and Abram went down to Egypt to live there for a while because the famine was severe. As he was about to enter Egypt, he said to his wife Sarai, 'I know what a beautiful woman you are. When the Egyptians see you, they will say, "This is his wife." Then they will kill me but will let you live. Say you are my sister, so that I will be treated well for your sake and my life will be spared because of you.'

When Abram came to Egypt, the Egyptians saw that she was a very beautiful woman. And when Pharaoh's officials saw her, they praised her to Pharaoh, and she was taken into his palace. He treated Abram well for her sake, and Abram acquired sheep and cattle, male and female donkeys, menservants and maidservants, and camels.

But the Lord inflicted serious diseases on Pharaoh and his household because of Abram's wife Sarai. So Pharaoh summoned Abram. 'What have you done to me?' he said. 'Why didn't you tell me she was your wife? Why did you say, "She is my sister," so that I took her to be my wife? Now then, here is your wife. Take her and go!' **Genesis 12:10-19**

Spiritual giants don't come any taller than Abraham, but, faced with pressure, he would sometimes distort the truth. Confronted by challenging circumstances, he would yield to self-preservation and deceive his way out of his difficulties.

He may have:

- believed God more than his present reality.

- looked forward to a city with foundations.

- fathered a child at the age of 100, by a barren woman.

- loved God more than his only son.

But he was still a liar. Yet God chose to use him powerfully.

**Liam has also been a liar**. This is his story.

He is an honest man with a criminal past. That is the positive spin. He is equally a criminal who is presently clean. At the age of 38 he surveys a life of anger, deception and impressive success. To date, he has spent much of his time in legal escapology. But the law from which he is running is relatively obscure. Not for him a dramatic retreat from the more obvious sanctions against theft, assault or deception. This is a man haunted by a statute which appears at the foot of many job application forms. Mention the Rehabilitation of Offenders Act (ROA) to Liam and watch his eyes fill with panic and his

Sweet tale: Liam's story of being haunted by the past.

pale face drain to shroud-white.

For good reason. Liam has risen through the ranks of the nursing profession by deliberately flouting the ROA. Moreover, he is a psychiatric nurse, an expert navigator of other people's minds. Here is a man who spends hours in the presence of obsession, panic, depression, mental collapse. He is very good at his job. But he is a chameleon, adept at disguise.

Liam's crisis is very adult. He is plagued by **unfinished business** in his youth, hamstrung by decisions he can barely remember. The words of the song are long forgotten but the gnawing tune goes on and on. Every day. You may have a great deal in common with Liam. Perhaps you:

- made adolescent decisions you deeply regret.

- thought you could get away with it.

- have to face the lonely truth.

- know more about anxiety than liberation.

This is his point of arrival. One day Liam decides to bare his soul to his employers. He determines to tell the truth about his lies. It's the end of a long process, but his many paths have dissolved into a single narrow track. No reversing. No overtaking. He will end this journey, and he expects it to be as sweet as death. But remember this — here is a man who, most of his life, has craved rehabilitation. Longing for acceptance, belonging, maturity, he lovingly fingers the self-destruct button.

He knows that his revelation will result in **instant dismissal**. Convinced of it. Driving to work that day, he has remembered to carry enough change for the bus fare home. His company car will be returned immediately and he will join the queue along with all the other car-less pedestrians. He parks, his clean shirt already sodden with fear and his heart beating a dangerous rhythm. Walking the long corridor to the office of the Director of Nursing Services, he fails to acknowledge the presence of other colleagues. Trapped in his own net, his mind swirls down into the old maelstroms.

Nothing unusual about his life. In fact it's unusually stable. Liam has had the same parents all his life and he comes from a large family. He also had a predisposition to:

truancy
  petty crime
    anger against authority
      unhappiness

All very normal. Liam left school without a single qualification, wandered around Britain with his girlfriend and finally settled down to a life of homelessness in Peterborough. Eventually his pregnant girlfriend moved back home with her parents and Liam spent his life boozing, begging and searching for food in dustbins.

At some point in most people's lives, there comes a moment of good fortune. Perhaps you're left a considerable amount of money. Or you meet someone who makes an appreciable difference. Liam met someone. He can't even remember the guy's name, but it was someone who arranged for him to stay in a builders' hostel.

It was raw. These men drank even harder than they worked, and they were expert at spotting a sucker. Someone who would pay their laundry bills. Liam, still only 18, was self-consciously worldly — but nothing prepared him for foul linens. His fellow residents spent each evening bingeing on spirits, lager and warm beer. They returned to the hostel to sleep soundly, frequently urinating and defecating in their beds. Here's the rub. Whenever this happened — and it was at least once a week — Liam's room was broken into and his clean laundry

> At some point in most people's lives, there comes a moment of good fortune.

exchanged for a pile of fetid sheets. On Fridays, the men returned to their homes for the weekend and the laundry was collected for cleaning. It was a free service — except when laundry had been deliberately soiled. Liam faced a large bill every weekend.

But it was an address. This opened up to him the wonderful world of state benefits and work training. After a few abortive job-tasting weeks, Liam was stroked by more luck. A wise DSS supervisor suggested he try his hand in a hospital for the mentally disabled. All his life Liam had also felt like an outsider, so he agreed. But first there was the simple procedural matter of completing an application form. Name, address, interests ... Rehabilitation of Offenders Act. What did that mean? He must declare any previous criminal convictions. Must reveal the string of minor convictions — the stolen bread rolls, the bottles smuggled ineffectually inside a baggy raincoat, the shop doorway trading in soft drugs.

'I'm crippled by life. I'm not rehabilitated. **I'll never get anywhere** if I tell them I'm a mess.'

So he lied. No convictions, no problems.

He was hooked from the first day. 'I felt like I belonged in all that noise and chaos.' Care assistants have a career ladder and Liam climbed quickly. No academic qualifications, but he worked hard and applied himself to his new life.

Which was when he met Mick the Vic, a local vicar. But a vicar with a difference. Mick suffered from severe epilepsy and, though it was medically controlled, he had no parish. Liam is convinced that epileptic clergymen are barred from parish ministry. Whether or not this is true, this is Liam's conclusion.

Mick was the hospital chaplain. 'He was a cross between Worzel Gummidge and Catweazle.' This cleric administered Holy Communion in council flats, baked bread for the women

I felt like I belonged...

of Greenham Common and delighted in fooling around with the patients in his care. And each summer, he and Liam took two of the most severely disabled away on a two-week holiday.

While Mick was a man of God, Liam refused to acknowledge God's existence. Human problems demanded a human solution. Godtalk merely produced unnecessary head pain.

By this time Liam was married and had two children. **A titanic situation**, soon to disappear. He left his family — tired, despondent, aching with self-pity. Moving into the hospital, he worked even harder, alienating himself from Mick and other friends. To cut a long story short:

- Liam left his wife and they divorced.

- He met a woman whom he would eventually marry.

- She encouraged him to train as a nurse.

- He did.

Liam opted for psychiatric training, but still the first academic hurdle had to be crossed. He had nothing to show for his twentysomething years, apart from several scars, tattoos and a tormented expression. Most people don't succeed in this national IQ test. Most people leave disappointed, nursing dreams shredded by clever questions. But not Liam. He passed and was offered training and a job.

What about the Rehabilitation of Offenders Act? Liam was angry. This clause, at the foot of every application form, infuriated him. He felt dislocated, out of sorts, alienated. He wanted desperately to be rehabilitated, but he knew that any honesty on his part would prevent him becoming a nurse and result in severe penalties for lying on all the other application forms.

So he lied. **Yet again**.

A second marriage ensued. Eventually, there were two more children. And the usual domestic traffic of house-buying, moving, financial worries, awful neighbours. More financial worries.

Parallel with regular upward promotion, life took a downward turn. 'There was something on my back.' Liam was on the verge of mental exhaustion, stressed out by his world. But Emma, his wife, was tasting faith. An exasperated Liam told her, 'This isn't right. I'm the psychiatrist. No God is going to help us.'

Unpaid bills and mortgage arrears brought possible bankruptcy. So they moved out and found rented accommodation before their credit record was mutilated by financial institutions.

Emma's emergent faith exploded into life. She joined a church and talked of 'asking Jesus into my life'. Irritated, embarrassed husband. Their agnostic confederation blown apart by Emma's appetite for God.

Her church minister, Nick, sought Liam's professional advice concerning one of his members.

> They became good friends
> river walking, often up to their necks
> hours of conversation on politics
> sport
> frequently religion

Liam decided to attend Alpha, an introductory course to the Christian faith. There he was deeply moved by the session on prayer. So moved, he tried it out for himself.

Taking an afternoon off, he quieted himself in a stain-glassed side-chapel in a nearby cathedral. Kneeling, sitting, shuffling anxiously. Nothing. He stood up and began to pace around the block floor. Nothing. Finally, 'I know you're there, but I need proof!' he exclaimed to the surprised altar. Silence, yes, but the silence following an explosion — `'I know you're there.'` Everything was changing...

- 'I believe, help thou my unbelief!' (the Bible).

- 'Thou has made us for thyself and our hearts are restless until they find their rest in thee' (St Augustine).

- The heart has its reasons...

- Faith seeks understanding.

Liam told Nick, invited Jesus Christ into his life and was baptised in the river where he walked.

'But I am still **not rehabilitated.**'

He was chewed up with it. The afterglow of faith was no consolation. Christianity was all well and good, but there were weighty matters of honesty and integrity to be traversed. Old feelings of panic prevented sleep, hindered eating, produced a constant state of perspiration. Would he finally come clean? If he did, he'd lose his job, home, reputation. Poverty, misery. But he had to do it. Compelled by some self-destructive righteousness, he plotted his course.

He's walking down the corridor, drenched in fear. She's not there, even though the appointment was made ten days ago. She's been called to an urgent management meeting. Liam begins to tell his tale of deception to her deputy and watches the sudden rush of blood away from her face. A call is made to the director, urging her to leave the meeting. She does and listens impassively to her employee's cascading honesty.

'You've got no choice. I know what the Act says. You must dismiss me.'

Phone calls must be made, colleagues consulted, the head of personnel sought. 'Liam, would you mind going for a walk and coming back in two hours?'

It's a long time waiting for the executioner, but the moment of judgement comes. 'She sat there like a poker player. I didn't know what she was thinking.' Momentous words flow.

'We **believe in rehabilitation**. You've been an excellent nurse for eighteen years and we're not going to lose you now. Your honesty has saved you.'

# chapter 6: the end doesn't have to be worse than the beginning

And what more shall I say? I do not have time to tell about Gideon... **Hebrews 11:32**

But I do have time. Gideon was an angry young man, who looked back in anger and detested his family's departure from faith. Living in a time of religious compromise, he despaired that his father had built an asherah pole in their backyard.

South Pole and North Pole I know, but asherah pole?

An asherah was a wooden, vertical carving used to worship pagan gods. It was believed that this tall, erectile statue had something to do with fertilising female gods, thus ensuring a good harvest.

Gideon, the youngest member of an anonymous family, decided to sabotage his father's beliefs. One night in the deadest hours, he vandalised his family's god, uprooting and upending the unfortunate pole. Despite this treachery, Gideon became a national hero, leading the people to a fantastic victory against the Amalekites. But at the end of his life he grew like his father, imposing meaningless beliefs on those around him:

And he said, 'I do have one request, that each of you give me an ear-ring from your share of the plunder.' (It was the custom of the Ishmaelites to wear gold ear-rings.)

They answered, 'We'll be glad to give them.' So they spread out a garment, and each man threw a ring from his plunder onto it. The weight of the gold rings he asked for came to seventeen hundred shekels, not counting the ornaments, the pendants and the purple garments worn by the kings of Midian or the chains that were on their camels' necks. Gideon made the gold into an ephod, which he placed in Ophrah, his town. All Israel prostituted themselves by worshipping it there, and it became a snare to Gideon and his family. **Judges 8:24-27**

Even worse than this, after his death the people reverted to the same nonsense that had originally ensnared his dad:

No sooner had Gideon died than the Israelites again prostituted themselves to the Baals. They set up Baal-Berith as their god and did not remember the LORD their God, who had rescued them from the hands of all their enemies on every side. **Judges 8:33-34**

In spite of an excellent beginning, Gideon finished badly. As a young man, faith in God had torched him. But in his old age, he reverted to the decadent and pointless spirituality of his ancestors.

Simon had a false start and was nearly disqualified, but he's **finishing strong**. So let me tell you Simon and Sadie's sweet tale.

**Sweet tale: Simon's addiction takes him to God's grace.**

It comes to a head the night he lies in his own blood, coughing, paralysed on one side. His wife and father-in-law stare numbly at the crumpled heap lying on the lounge carpet. First light, and Simon is twitching in his fluids, groaning for release.

Simon is an employee of a large company, father to two children and a keen Christian, until recently a regular and much appreciated preacher at their church. He's also a drug addict.

Sadie's and Stan's passivity is not down to a lack of compassion. Simply, they have seen it all before. It has happened once too often and they don't know what to do next. Simon is a short, solid, physically compressed man. Not easy to lift, but they do, driving him to the nearest Accident and Emergency.

Rewind. Simon grew up under his grandmother's shadow. She lived with the family and she was hooked on Valium. Long-time depressive illness had made her an NHS junkie in a period when prescriptions lasted for years. During his adolescence Simon began to develop headaches, like many young people. In a desire to help her young grandson, she gave him some of her tablets. As the headaches increased, so did his Valium consumption. Within months he'd come to suckle on the pills' impact. Within a couple of years **he was ensnared**.

His young adult life was flavoured by Pentecostal Christianity, falling in love with Sadie and a descent into the twilight world of soft drugs. During their courtship and the first few months of marriage he succeeded in concealing his addiction. Moderately successful at work, zealous at church, prowling the streets late at night to score. Soft became hard when valium gave way to cannabis, then crack, smack and speed. Culminating in heroin. By the time he'd turned hard, he had lost any desire to conceal his poisonous habit, oblivious to the anguish of his wife and family.

At the A&E, Simon makes a giant decision — he accepts that he needs help. Sadie knows of a Christian drug rehabilitation community and books him in. His addiction has left them exhausted and in serious debt.

Arriving at the community, Simon and Sadie are shown their new home — a caravan with no running water. Sadie's intention is to return home and restore stability to their three children, but the community's leadership insists that she stay and support Simon in his recovery. 'It was awful. I've never been through a more painful time. I felt dead inside, numb, but I couldn't stop crying. I'd wake up every morning to a soaking pillow, my face raw with tears. I simply couldn't stop weeping, although inside I felt emotionally dead.' While her mind takes a respite, her heart fragments. Moistly quiet.

After several weeks of promises, no baths and greasy hair, Simon breaks into the main house's mains supply and runs a pipe to the caravan.

Crisis makes victims and heroes of us all, and Sadie is a heroine. She stood by her drug-drunk husband as he drove his family to the brink of insolvency and her through a living nightmare. During their few years at the community, Simon experiences a profound miracle. `Christians call it grace`. Escaping from people whose version of Christianity contained authoritarianism and legalism, his healing happens in their damp caravan.

'I came to realise that only God could do it. I'd lost everything, and couldn't hide any more. Faith, life, kicking my toxic habits, could only be received as a gift from God. I realised that all my life I'd thought of myself as a piece of rubbish, and I ended up abusing myself and everyone close to me. God showed me how much he loved me and valued my love. I saw Jesus in a new way, and he gave me the strength to pull through.'

After their time in the community, Simon and Sadie move to a neighbouring village and live in rented accommodation. Their children attend the local school and they are involved in a nearby church. A few years later and you'll find them fifty miles up the motorway, leading a new church. A journey which started in the mess of addiction is ending in the order of love.

# chapter 7: twelve steps to heaven

> Now faith is being sure of what we hope for and certain of what we do not see. This is what the ancients were commended for. **Hebrews 11:1-2**

Hope is always in the future, a belief that the time yet to be contains a preferable scenario. Christians have always been guilty of hope. Not all Christians — some are as miserable as everyone else. But many are, and have been, crazy optimists.

Jesus believed that the joy stretching out before him was so wonderful, he endured the gibbet. Endured it, mark you, in a state of nakedness. Not merely emotional or mental vulnerability, but literal nudity. This was part of the Roman Empire's torture package: maximum physical pain and maximum humiliation. The body's gradual disfigurement through impalement and all the unpleasant side-effects were evident to everyone.

Paul, who wrote a large chunk of the New Testament, was another **hope junkie**. Even though other people regarded him as having amazing faith and courage, he knew a different story. He knew that some of his attitudes, motivations and habits were not honouring to God. In struggling with his own sinfulness, he felt as though he was strapped to a body of death.

> What a wretched man I am! Who will rescue me from this body of death? Thanks be to God — through Jesus Christ our Lord! **Romans 7:24**

**Body of death?** As though he were strapped to a dead body, whose decay would eventually eat away at his healthy tissue and organs. This is a statement of addiction, helplessness in the face of moral and spiritual corrosion.

And yet...

Though they go mad they shall be sane,
Though they sink through the sea they shall
        rise again;
Though lovers be lost love shall not;
And death shall have no dominion.
Dylan Thomas

If there is no hope, there is addiction. An addict is someone who feels abandoned by the future and sucks on the present — and so becomes yesterday's woman, yesterday's man. Intoxicated by the past's poison, the addict seeks comfort through God's good gifts. But it's a disfigured excellence — alcohol, sex, medicine, food ... mutilated by gross need.

'I was a defect looking for a character,' is **Billy's** semi-humorous assessment of his former addiction. But how do you become an alcoholic? Try mixing generous amounts of bad fathering and wretched family life, add to it powerful feelings of failure and self-pity, give it a good stir and wait for the damaged life to rise.

Well, sometimes, but not always. Some people just seem to be born that way, and there are many cases where there is no obvious reason for the growth of crippling addiction in a person's life.

Sweet tale: Billy — 'I was a defect looking for a character.'

Billy is such a person. Growing up in postwar Taunton, he merged with the working-class culture of the day: rock 'n' roll, Brylcreem, and 1950s affluence jangling in his pockets. Nothing unusual about his upbringing, neither demons nor angels. Except that **the world of language was chaotic** and there was no name for it.

'When I was eleven years old, nobody knew about being dyslexic. Nobody knew about that word. You were just thick. You were given the dunce cap and put in the corner.'

In his eleventh year, during yet another day of humiliating absence from school, there was a knock on the door. It was the man from the Education Board, intruding upon Billy's mother trying to teach him to write his name. He went away and reported this to his superiors. 'And the next minute they sent me to the psychiatrist, and then they decided to send me away to a special school in Gloucester, which was for maladjusted children.'

He returned to Taunton aged fifteen. And he began to drink. And drink. But strangely, despite a culture which has made victims of us all, Billy doesn't blame his background for his alcoholism. He puts it all down to **chemistry**. As far as Billy is concerned — indeed, as far as AA is concerned — alcoholism is an allergic reaction to alcohol. No more, no less.

'I would be in the pub, and I would say to myself, "It's nine o' clock, I'll go home"; but I never did. I was always the last one there. And I would wake up putting the key in the door, having blacked out. And then wake up the next morning full of guilt and remorse, saying, "It will never happen again." Then two days later I'd be going out and doing the same things again.'

Billy's life was totally **defined by drink**: his career as a merchant seaman, his wedding day, the birth of his sons, everyday life. Alcoholism eventually robbed him of his wife and boys and, as he tells his story, his West Country baritone burr breaks as he calls to mind the fear and distress that once cloaked his home life. He eventually ended up in a local mental hospital.

My idea of God when I was drinking was of an old man in a long cloak and beard, writing dirty things in a book about me, and he was never going to forgive me.

Billy downed his last drink on 30 January 1985, on the way to getting a haircut. Finding the barbers full, he visited a nearby hotel bar and, as usual, stayed there all day. The following morning, waking to an empty house, he was consumed, again, by guilt and began thinking about God. 'My idea of God when I was drinking was of an old man in a long cloak and beard, writing dirty things in a book about me, and he was never going to forgive me.'

He didn't want to be alone, so he rang his sister who came and took him to her house. From there, he rang AA and, within the hour, three local members visited him. That night he went to his first AA meeting. He attended 123 meetings in as many days.

Eighteen months later he was still dry but on the verge of committing suicide. No one told him how he could change on the inside. Behaviour is one thing, personality is quite another, and all the talk in AA of God or a higher power just wasn't helping him.

It was then that he encountered Clarence Snyder. Snyder was one of the founders of AA, who believed that faith in Christ was the only means of living an addiction-free life. Billy listened to his testimony on tape and later rang Florida to learn more, only to discover that Snyder had died in 1984. But Snyder had established an annual spiritual retreat in Florida based on the twelve steps of AA. Billy visited Florida and met many men whose encounter with Christ had **transformed** their lives. 'They were alcoholics, they put hands on me, and I was filled with the Holy Spirit.' He returned home, a changed man, eager to share his new faith with fellow alcoholics and eager for baptism.

Several trips to Florida now ensued. He and his newly reconciled wife attended several retreats and felt that this Christianised version of the Twelve Steps could work in

Somerset. So, in 1993, a group came over from Florida and held their first ever retreat for alcoholics in an abbey deep in the South Devon countryside. Since then they have held them twice yearly, with men and women coming from all over Europe to attend. People desperate to seek the power of Christ to kick their addiction. Billy and seven other Christian alcoholics went on to establish a branch of AA founded on explicitly Christian principles.

One man's meat may be another man's poison, but in Billy's case his old poison is helping him minister spiritual medicine to many others.

There may be three steps to heaven, but it takes twelve to get to recovery. The club based on twelve steps ranks among the most well known in the world. According to Sir Anthony Hopkins, it is the best club in the world and the best party in town. A self-confessed alcoholic, this Oscar-winning actor makes a point of attending AA meetings wherever he is, be it London, Lagos or LA.

Alcoholism, like every other addiction, is no respecter of culture, gender or national boundaries and — like the church — is to be found just about everywhere you go. AA did not begin simply as a human response to a human need. It was born out of the transforming experiences of two alcoholics who came to faith in Christ.

The key text in the young movement's history is The Twelve Steps — simple to understand, brutally honest and offering a classic definition of the addict's cry. They're worth a closer look:

We...

1  Admitted we were powerless over alcohol — that our lives had become unmanageable.

2 Came to believe that a Power greater than ourselves could restore us to sanity.

3 Made a decision to turn our will and our lives over to the care of God as we understood him.

4 Made a searching and fearless moral inventory of ourselves.

5 Admitted to God, to ourselves, and to another human being the exact nature of our wrongs.

6 Were entirely ready to have God remove all these defects of character.

7 Humbly asked him to remove our shortcomings.

8 Made a list of all persons we had harmed, and became willing to make amends to them all.

9 Made direct amends to such people wherever possible, except when to do so would injure them or others.

10 Continued to take personal inventory and, when we were wrong, promptly admitted it.

11 Sought, through prayer and meditation, to improve our conscious contact with God as we understood him, praying only for knowledge of his will for us and the power to carry that out.

12 Having had a spiritual awakening as the result of these steps, we tried to carry this message to alcoholics, and to practise these principles in all our affairs.

The Twelve Steps has outgrown AA. All kinds of recovery groups use them extensively. Addiction's aroma is no longer confined to spirits, but to food, sex, drugs, gambling and work. We are all addicts these days. Fifty years ago, words such as *addict*, *abused*, *victim* were the currency of shame. But it's all changed now.

AA's God is whoever you perceive him to be. But here's the intriguing rub. In every AA meeting, there is a distant beat of the rhythm that pulses in the Bible: God loves sinners and God helps sinners. Sin is addiction and addiction is sin. Sin is a falling short of God's standards and it carries with it a compulsion to do it time after time. We are addicted to sin.

'Parts of my life are out of control.'

'I feel so guilty.'

'I try my best and I keep failing. How can I ever know that God still loves me?'

Jesus straightened up and asked her, 'Woman, where are they? Has no-one condemned you?'

'No-one, sir,' she said.

'Then neither do I condemn you,' Jesus declared. 'Go now and leave your life of sin.' John 8:10-11

You see, at just the right time, when we were still powerless, Christ died for the ungodly. Very rarely will anyone die for a righteous man, though for a good man someone might possibly dare to die. But God demonstrates his own love for us in this: While we were still sinners, Christ died for us. Romans 5:6-8

# chapter 8: lost in the crowd

By faith Abel offered God a better sacrifice than Cain did. By faith he was commended as a righteous man, when God spoke well of his offerings. And by faith he still speaks, even though he is dead. **Hebrews 11:4**

'It's me. Abel. I've been dead a long time, but you can still hear my voice. If you asked me why I died so violently, I would still have no answer. Cain and I were never the best of buddies, but we had the same blood and the same young history. I kept sheep and he farmed arable. He had a temper and I didn't.

'But there must have been more to it than that, although I've read that Bible passage many times and it still doesn't make any sense to me...'

Now Cain said to his brother Abel, 'Let's go out to the field.' And while they were in the field, Cain attacked his brother Abel and killed him. **Genesis 4:8**

'But I did have an apprehension of God, a kind of feeling for him. You must understand that we had no Bible then, and very few stories about him. Except that my parents were there from the beginning. They saw him face to face. Actually saw God, before they were driven from our home. Dad never spoke much about that — it hurt too much. In fact, the rest of his life was completely destroyed by regret and a yearning to meet the man he called "The Gardener".

'Dad's screwed-up regret never really polluted me, but it did Cain. He was mentally messed up by our father's bitter disappointment. I mean, every day he would lay into Mum, saying it was all her fault they had no real home, no fun in life. He felt very angry about it all, blaming my mother and God for everything. He believed in God, but argued that he was a cosmic sadist who delighted in ruining lives. I couldn't agree. I felt him to be a person of great beauty, and thinking of him brought me feelings of joy.

'Occasionally, when I was on my own, I would light a fire, build an altar and roast a lamb for him. It seemed right. The smoke would rise to the skies and was a way of telling him that I needed him. Cain hated that. Dad told us we had to worship him, but Cain did it grudgingly, bringing a few turnips and other veg. When he asked me why I was throwing good money after bad in sacrificing my lambs, I told him, "It's like the life in the lamb's blood is flowing for the bad feelings in our family." That was the last time we spoke.'

We move on, paying another visit to the AA meeting. People are shuffling through the main door and a group of friends are laughing near the kitchen hatch. Yellowing green paint peels like eczema from the walls, soothed only by condensation and steam. Chairs in an untidy series of concentric circles, are gradually filled by twos and threes, and some solitary figures.

A voice speaks. 'Hello, I'm Martin and I'm an alcoholic.' You could tell he was. Looked rough, flushed skin, wild eyes and torn clothes. Just what you'd expect.

Somebody else.

Sweet tales: The alcoholics seeking a higher power.

'Hello, I'm Moira and I'm an alcoholic. I'm a musician and I've made a lot of money out of it.' She had one of those — what do you call it? — cut-glass accents. Smart, well-dressed, pretty. Not what you'd expect.

'I was with the London Symphony Orchestra for several years, touring around the world. Different bed every night, sometimes a different country every night. I don't know how it happened, but I felt I couldn't get off the wheel, spinning faster and faster. I started drinking, just to `calm myself down` every night. Helped me sleep. Scotch mainly, and some wine. For some reason, it never seemed enough and I'd drink half a bottle regularly. Helped for a while, but the panic symptoms came back and I started drinking at lunchtimes and even in the mornings. In the end, I would keep a flask in my bag all the time and during every rehearsal break I'd nip out to the back for a drink. One day I collapsed and was rushed to hospital with chronic alcohol poisoning. I came to AA because a friend invited me and, for the first six months, someone rang me up every day to make sure I wasn't drinking. I've been dry now for three years, but I'm still an alcoholic.'

Applause. Silence. Then someone else gets to her feet. She's in her mid-thirties, also pretty — but sunken.

'I'm a mother of two children and I've always lived in this area. Don't know why, but I started drinking after my second girl was born. Doctors told me it was postnatal depression. Started taking sherry with my lunch, then it was lunch with my sherry. About tea time, before my husband came home, I'd open a bottle of wine and have a few glasses. Before long I was drinking a bottle of sherry a day. Vodka in the evening. I haven't had an unhappy life, but there came a time when `I just couldn't cope`. With anything. I'd wake up feeling panicky about the smallest things. Even taking my youngest to playgroup in the morning made me really stressed. A year ago I was rushed to hospital with alcohol poisoning. When I got home, my husband suggested I give AA a ring.

'I decided, "Enough is enough", and joined AA. I'm not particularly religious but I know there is a higher power who can help me. When you join, you're given a sponsor who looks after you and visits you at home. The one I had rang me up about six times a day for two years, checking that I hadn't drunk anything. If I was desperate for a drink or felt tempted, he'd come to see me straight away and talk me through it.

'I haven't touched a drop for ten years now, but I'm still an alcoholic. Today, I'm free of it. Tomorrow, who knows?'

Another woman stands up, a little older. Katie. 'To begin with I wasn't a great drinker, though I'd drink socially. Then financial pressure hit and I began to drink a little more than usual. I found rapidly that `I couldn't do without it`. Within a matter of weeks I needed medical help, and was told that I had a condition which meant that I craved alcohol but my craving was poisoning me. I went on the wagon and didn't miss it that much. I was careful to avoid situations where it might be available.

'Then the family were invited to a wedding. I felt very virtuous, didn't touch a drop all day. But I took one mouthful of the wedding cake and passed out. I was rushed to the local hospital. Discovered that there'd been spirits in the cake and this was enough to send my body into complete shock. I was in hospital longer this time, and was visited several times by the hospital chaplain. Talked, listened, chatted. He spoke about Jesus Christ in the present tense, not as a past figure. Gave me a few Bible verses which he thought might help.'

```
Here is my servant, whom I uphold,
    my chosen one in whom I delight;
I will put my Spirit on him
    and he will bring justice to the nations.
He will not shout or cry out,
    or raise his voice in the streets.
A bruised reed he will not break,
    and a smouldering wick he will not snuff out.
Isaiah 42:1-3
```

'The Spirit of the Lord is on me,
　　because he has anointed me
　　to preach good news to the poor.
He has sent me to proclaim freedom for the
　　　　prisoners
　　and recovery of sight for the blind,
to release the oppressed
　　to proclaim the year of the Lord's
　　　　favour.'

Then [Jesus] rolled up the scroll, gave it back to the attendant and sat down. The eyes of everyone in the synagogue were fastened on him, and he began by saying to them, 'Today this scripture is fulfilled in your hearing.' Luke 4:18-21

'For the first time in my life, I realised that faith was a living relationship with a real God who could help me. The chaplain put me in touch with AA and also a local church. I am now a Christian and, even though I still struggle with life, I know that Jesus is with me all the time, helping and guarding me.'

The meeting is over. As you scuttle away into the grey afternoon, you may feel a song rise up inside you. You may have been transfixed by the searing honesty of those who spoke, and have experienced a strange joy. 'Hello, I'm X, and I'm an alcoholic.' No pretence. No attempt to rationalise the situation, offer excuses or blame anyone else. No references to self-improvement. Most of them hadn't drunk alcohol in years and they could easily have sought to create a better impression by saying, 'I used to be such and such', or 'In the past I had this addiction but now I'm stronger.' None of it. 'I'm a **powerless** addict and I need a higher power to help me stay dry. Today I haven't touched a drop, but who knows about tomorrow?'

I wonder. How might this work in church? How might it be for a group of men to sit together on the basis of weakness — not fear masquerading as strength? Imagine an evening of storytelling, sharing the experiences of the week, each account prefaced by self-honesty. Not self-indulgence. Simply to acknowledge that you and I are held captive by many things, against which we feel **powerless**.

'Hello, I'm John and I've watched pornography this week. Like every other week.'

'Hello, I'm Martin, and I've been too busy for my children this week.'

'Hello, I'm Darren, and I'm in terrible debt and I can't get out of it.'

'Hello, I'm Peter, and I'm on the verge of having an affair with someone at work.'

'Hello, I'm Chris, and I can't stop insulting my wife.'

'Hello, I'm Andy, and I don't really love God any more.'

Hello. We are all addicts here.

Every form of addiction is bad, no matter whether the narcotic be alcohol or morphine or idealism.
Carl Gustav Jung

# chapter 9: weak strength

...who shut the mouths of lions, quenched the fury of the flames, and escaped the edge of the sword; whose weakness was turned to strength; and who became powerful in battle and routed foreign armies. Hebrews 11:33-34

**Samson had one bad-hair day** and it cost him his life. Dedicated at birth to be a Nazirite, he refused rich food and strong drink, preferring healthy diets and spiritual workouts. A fighter of bears, Samson's reputation as a warrior quickly became legendary. Curiously, his flowing mane was the focus of his strength. From birth, his mother vowed that his hair would never be cut, and it never was. Until he met Delilah.

This non-Jewish woman intoxicated Samson with her beauty, resulting in seduction and tragedy. Even though he was already married, he gave himself to her, compromising his faith and family. His Philistine enemies bribed Delilah to discover the secret of his great strength. She succeeded — as he slept, his head was shaved:

Then she called, 'Samson, the Philistines are upon you!'

He awoke from his sleep and thought, 'I'll go out as before and shake myself free.' But he did not know that the LORD had left him.

Then the Philistines seized him, gouged out his eyes and took him down to Gaza. Binding him

Sweet tale: Tom
- different,
thrilled by the
risks, heavy
with the guilt.

with bronze shackles, they set him to grinding in the prison. **Judges 16:20-21**

**Tom has known social privilege** for most of his life. His father is a senior executive in a multinational oil company, and he has lived in some of the world's wealthiest and most exotic countries. He received a better than average education — good GCSEs and A levels, degree in music, further academic studies. He's zany, good-looking, clever, amusing and dangerously out of control. And get this, as he takes the spotlight, he has the most amazing head of hair. Poor little rich kid?

This is Tom's story as he tells it himself.

I was sent away to public school at an early age and I've always felt different. **Always different**. From the beginning I was musical and theatrical. Loud voice but actually very private. When I was a teenager I was popular at school — loads of parties, loads of productions. For about four years I didn't know whether or not I was gay. Sometimes I'm still not sure. No friends, really. I mean, not really good mates who love you for who you are, whatever you've done. Although I've slept with quite a few people.

I started cutting out pictures of women in underwear, from catalogues I found in school. I'd hide them away in a toy postbox and take them out when I went to the toilet. I learnt to masturbate when I was 11. Looking back I think I was quite lonely. I was at a boys' school and for most of my adolescence couldn't work out if I was more attracted to boys or girls.

I had a few girl friends during the long holidays, but I also got involved with some of the boys at prep school and later at public school. You could say I was arty, but I also enjoyed football. Quite a lad, really. Eventually I was sent to another school, to study for my GCSEs and A levels. I really hated it. I missed my parents terribly, even though they lived all over the place. They moved every couple of years, so home as a place just didn't exist. It was round about this time that I felt that I couldn't control my sexuality. I'd be in a lesson, like English, and I'd get an urge to masturbate. Most people, if they feel like that, don't do anything about it ... think about something else. Not me. I started masturbating during lessons. No one ever noticed what I was doing, and I didn't do it every lesson. But it became a regular habit. Part of the thrill was the danger of getting caught. Strange really, it wasn't just about lust. It was as much the thrill of the risk.

I was having more sexual liaisons now. It was a mixed school and we were allowed quite a lot of freedom. I had a sexual relationship with another boy who was part of the school orchestra. We didn't have intercourse, but we did just about everything else. I was also very attracted to girls and went out with a few during my time there.

But something was happening in my mind. During my involvements with other people, or even on my own, a kind of paralysis would creep over me. Like being out of control and feeling I was looking on at someone else. I would often feel as though these extreme situations weren't happening to me. Yes, looking on at somebody else's mess. I can't explain it, except that everything seemed grey, twisted, horrid and tantalising. I don't think of myself as a sexual freak, but I know that I'm intoxicated by that feeling of menace.

I can't honestly say that religion, or Christianity, played a large part in my life. I'd been confirmed and went to church every Sunday during term time, but none of it made a great deal of sense. Except that I did feel guilty a lot of the time. But since Christianity offered few answers and nothing better, I carried on as I was.

I left school and studied music at an arts college. Those few years were to change everything and nothing. I got involved with a group of people who were self-confessed Christians. I'd never met anyone who'd ever admitted to this before. To my way of thinking, to be a Christian was to be white, male and Anglo-Saxon. Not a label I was proud to own, especially in front of others. But these people were different. They liked the music I listened to, laughed a great deal, cooked badly, and spoke a language of faith. Their vocabulary revolved around love, forgiveness, transparency and God. I couldn't quite figure it, because they wore my clothes and hummed my tunes, but God to them was a source of intense joy and curiosity. After a while I went to their prayer gatherings and even to their church.

The Jesus I was introduced to was unlike the one I had previously encountered. During my school days, I regarded Jesus Christ as **a kind of senior prefect** who, if anything, was always disapproving. Most of the time he simply didn't have a say. If I had any thoughts about his crucifixion, it was a kind of ghastly bewilderment at such meaningless agony. I couldn't understand why so many hymns revelled in such a sadistic event.

But this was different. Jesus was spoken of as a saviour and healer. He was presented as a man who identified with sin — my sin. Unlike the Jesus of my schooldays, he understood my twisted, tormented needs and desired to pour in his unusual salve. And the cross was no enigmatic meat-hook. This was offered to me as a place of unique glory, a locus of mercy. Jesus of Nazareth identifying with the screwed-up offspring of Adam, bearing their brokenness and dishing out the forgiveness of heaven. And all in love, the greatest of motives.

There came a moment when he seemed to me so real and immediate, that I wanted to turn away from my darkness and confess him and him alone as my Saviour, Lord and healer. I was baptised and became part of my friends' church. Everything had changed.

Until. Dissonant, angry chords returned to my mind. The old score started playing in my head, except this time it was more brutal and portentous. I fought it for a while, pleading the name of Jesus, attending meetings, reading the Bible. All this helped, but dark promises and wild fruit now filled my horizon.

I scanned the classified pages of a local newspaper and visited a few massage parlours. I went a few times to different establishments. The girls there do whatever you ask them to, and you pay for it. No one gets hurt. Not enough danger, but **the guilt was colossal**. This time, it was informed guilt and not some religious chamber of horrors. I had wounded my Jesus and let my friends down.

I confessed my sin to my pastor and friends. They prayed with me, applauded my honesty and it helped. For a while.

Then one day, I was on my way to college, walking up a quiet lane when I felt the need to masturbate in public. There was nobody around, so I did it as I walked along. Just as I came, a car appeared round the corner. I managed to conceal what I was doing. I could have got into big trouble.

Fast track to nowhere. Like others, I guess, I became a tale of two visors. My days became marked by the lack of control I thought I had abandoned. Sexual need and barbed-wire thrills made their reappearance, offering a foaming and dangerous cocktail.

My life each day revolved around my next secret. There were times when I'd be consumed with sexual need. Very frightening. And exhilarating.

I knew a local businessman who died trying to get a few kicks. It's all about timing. Suitable placing of a piece of wire,

...each day revolved around my next secret.

a length of rope and an orange, and then you switch the electricity on. Mild shock. Amazing orgasm. So they say. I've thought a lot about doing it.

Things came to a head after a brief fling with a girl in my college year. Bizarrely, it didn't start off as sex. Her boyfriend had left her and she was almost suicidal. I listened, comforted, even prayed with her. A casual embrace gave way to more intimate touching and eventually full intercourse. Within a couple of weeks she told me she was pregnant. Fear, terror, bitter regret. It turned out she was wrong, but I felt my chaotic behaviour had caught up with me.

There were other episodes, with other people, over a period of a year. I tired of the never-ending round of tell-and-forgiveness sessions. So did everyone else. One by one, my friends, the pastor, other church members listened to me and laid their love on me. But they began to go further:

'Tom, this can't carry on.'

'Who has got the most power in your life?'

'What's the point of following Jesus if you live this kind of life?'

'Your life could be very different to this.'

I made myself accountable to a number of people. I met with them twice a week and they would ask me blunt, direct questions. I determined to let the Bible do something new in me. I knew that the Spirit of God could renew my mind, transform me even, and I decided that I would make this my goal.

I completed my degree and embarked on a specialist music course in another city. Joined a new church, made different friends, tried to live a new life. I still mess up from time to time, but my appetites are renewing. **The taste of normality is wonderful.**

# chapter 10: scarlet rope

By faith the prostitute Rahab, because she welcomed the spies, was not killed with those who were disobedient. **Hebrews 11:31**

Rahab was a prostitute. A Canaanite hooker. Not only was she not Jewish, she also earned her money by means of the filthiest profession known to the Hebrew people. She lived in the city of Jericho.

At the time the Israelites were planning to destroy Jericho as part of their strategy to conquer the land God had promised would be theirs. The Israelite leader, Joshua, instructed a couple of spies to enter the city and report their findings. During their espionage they were offered hospitality by Rahab, who protected them when they were pursued by the men sent by the king of Jericho to find them. She also revealed that she knew the purpose of their mission:

Before the spies lay down for the night ... [Rahab] said to them, 'I know that the LORD has given this land to you and that a great fear of you has fallen on us, so that all who live in this country are melting in fear because of you ... everyone's courage failed because of you, for the LORD your God is God in heaven above and on the earth below. Now then, please swear to me by the LORD that you will show kindness to my family, because I have shown kindness to you. Give me a sure sign that you will spare the lives of my father and mother, my brothers and sisters, and all who belong to them, and that you will save us from death.' Joshua 2:8-9,11-13

Q: And the sign is?

A: A scarlet rope that she must tie to an upstairs window. When seen, the marauding Israelites would leave her home untouched.

Some names give away their period. Maud, Dora, Sybil speak of Edwardian England. Harry, Charlie and Sophie are having a renaissance following an absence of two generations. But what can be said of Sandy? This is a name which exudes the Swinging Sixties. Sandy summons up mini-skirts, hair lacquer, shiny plastic and G-plan furniture.

**Sandy** is a Sixties girl. To meet her is to encounter Carnaby Street, Mary Quant and Marianne Faithfull. And like many of her contemporaries she bears generational scars. A string of broken relationships, violent partners, lonely years and chronic fatigue bear witness to the period's social and moral upheaval. She's always been an activist — her feet hardened by regular pilgrimages in the company of other political monks: CND, Greenpeace, Friends of the Earth. Undergirding it all was a political and spiritual framework which commanded almost total loyalty and fervour.

Sandy is vivid, sparkling, alive. She became a Christian in her late thirties, and her extrovert personality means that those who meet her become acquainted with this fact very quickly. Her love of God is passionate, outspoken and experimental. Having tasted the sweetness of God after much bitterness, she is clear in her beliefs and determined to make the Bible's picture of God her own. She needs to. Surveying a past of drug dealers and small-time British Mafiosi, she has come to love the face of God.

Sweet tale:
Sandy — bearer
of scars,
passionate about
Jesus.

Meet her today. She lives in a modest home, simply decorated. Confident, in control, outgoing. Happily married, eager labrador, committed to her local church. It's **a picture of wholeness**.

But not always. Turn the clock back fifteen years. Home is a cramped flat in the middle of Swansea, shared with a couple of vein-and-needle experts. But in reality, home is even smaller than it appears. Confined to her bed for most of the day, Sandy is racked with physical and emotional pain, weeping, often uncontrollably. Separated from her husband, she fears that she has no future. She has been married three times and bears the emotional bruises. Relationships that involved infidelity — theirs as well as hers. Violence, abuse, anger, fear — these have been her relational staple-diet most of her life.

In middle age as in youth, she appears a smouldering beauty, full of sexual electricity. Reality transcends this. Sandy longs to know and be known. Weary of political and marital frenzy, her mind and body have begun to break down. Medicine offers little support and she turns towards New Age remedies: therapy groups, alternative health clinics. Messy divorce has left her penniless and rootless. Her move to West Wales has no motive other than the desire to escape. A chance conversation in a pub leads to Bleak House. Actually, it's a flat. Confined to bed, she abandons herself to a culture of dirty needles, decaying take-away food and the random migrations of her flatmates' visitors. Not only does she not feel any better, she begins to apprehend **a personal sense of evil** in her life.

It happened like this. In the stark oasis of her room, she notices that the noises off from the lounge change. On top of the chillingly cool ambient sounds, human voices prevail. References to tarot cards are heard, astrological charts plotted, and odd chanting. She becomes aware of someone in her room

**Pieces of furniture untouched by human hands fall and break.**

— a presence with no body but alarmingly real. Pieces of furniture untouched by human hands fall and break. Her own body is touched as though by an ancient incubus. She learns later of her co-habitees' fondness for astral travel. Sandy doesn't believe in God or the devil, but she recognises that she has encountered a reality beyond her understanding.

Her perceptions of Christianity are not favourable, scorched with allegations of hypocrisy and irrelevance. Christians are only interested in themselves and in keeping up an image of good behaviour. Sandy wants more. She wants life — and it's killing her.

A group of people move from the shadows into her domain. She has known most of them for years, but they live miles away. She makes a few calls and they turn up on the same day, converging from various locations. **They are all on her side**. Oddly, they are all Christians — followers, as far as she is concerned, of a discredited way. They are:

- her sister-in-law, someone she has long respected as being different to other churchgoers in her family.

- a friend she secretly admires for her integrity.

- a struggling artist she doesn't know very well, a man who believes that God restores broken lives.

- a magazine editor, whose particular brand of Christianity she is suspicious of, but nevertheless she 'likes his karma', as she puts it.

Through prayer, conversation and care, this odd crowd introduces her to Jesus. Friend of sinners, mender of broken lives, Saviour of the world. Jesus, whose fragrance to her is fresh, not oozing the mothballs of ecclesiastical history. Confronted by his love for her and her need of change and forgiveness, she asks him to forgive her and enter her life. She becomes a Christian. Shortly afterwards, she spends a day in **e c s t a s y**, when his presence is so sweet and immediate that she feels consumed by him. For the first time in ages she begins to feel valued and loved.

This, however, is no tale of triumphant victory. Sandy's health remains poor and family relationships strained. But her confession is very clear. There was a time when she was ignorant of Christ, a stranger to his loving presence. She now knows that she is part of his family. As far as she can, she throws herself into her new church, charming many with her bubbly faith and irritating others with her uncompromising theology.

In tandem with her new faith are days of terrible darkness. Sleepless months, night-time fear, aching limbs. She seeks counsel from other Christians and receives prayer. She begins to believe that her crippling malaise is due to the evil presence in her life. She embarks on a lengthy course of prayer with others, seeking to expel the darkness within by calling on the name of Jesus.

The years accelerate. She moves to Cardiff and rents a place of her own. Her physical condition improves and she grows spiritually by numerous leaps. But still she feels pressed in by her emotional and mental struggles. Outwardly, she presents herself as dynamic, purposeful, extrovert. Inwardly, she is **howling for release**. Days of faith and intimacy with God give way to terrifyingly dark periods of fear and loneliness — a colossal struggle between her creative and pastoral instincts and the urge to curl up in bed never to emerge again.

Then Stephen arrives. He's been in her orbit for some years — a friend of a friend. Stephen is a quiet, unassuming, attractively insecure fortysomething. Inheritor of a prim English upbringing and an Oxford University degree, he is the epitome of reserve and tact. Combined with his agnosticism, he is the exact opposite to Sandy's hot outlook.

He is, however, no stranger to Christianity. Committed to the pursuit of ideas and free thought, he has been part of a Bible-study group run by one of the other local churches. The group was a mixture of committed Christians and curious non-Christians. As they worked their way through the four Gospels, Stephen enjoyed the discussions, the expressed faith of some of the men and the male banter. After several months the group disbanded. He left a changed man, but not in the way you might imagine. He wasn't a Christian, joined no church and continued to believe in his agnosticism. Except this — through his attendance and the ambience of faith and free enquiry, something of God's presence had rubbed off on him.

Then they met — Professor Higgins and Eliza Doolittle — at a Christmas party. And both were initially unimpressed. To her, he was aloof, a spectacled academic out of touch with his own feelings. To him, she was over the top, overwhelmingly emotional and appallingly certain of her Christian convictions. But within days they bumped into each other again, and she invited him to an event at her church. He was suspicious, but agreed. By this time she had begun to kindle his ardour and he was keen to know her more. Sandy's feelings towards Stephen were mixed. She didn't find him sexually attractive, but she was beginning to enjoy his company. And she could also see that he needed Jesus.

It's what the church calls 'a power night'. Interspersed between the big noise of a black gospel choir are the **high-octane personal stories**. People who've known the slavery of addiction speak out what Jesus has done for them. It's too much for Stephen. He storms out of the building, swearing that he will never again enter a church.

It's all useless. Sandy pursues him with Christianity and by now he's head over his heels in love with her. He goes to church with her again within a matter of weeks and this time is pleasantly and powerfully surprised. During the service a man shares his story of faith and he is touched. Later, the preacher speaks about Jesus and Zacchaeus the tax collector, during which he uses some poetic licence. 'In the same way that Jesus knew Zacchaeus's name before they actually met, he knows your name now. Stephen.'

Stephen – pursued, in love, and known by God.

Jesus entered Jericho and was passing through. A man was there by the name of Zacchaeus; he was a chief tax collector and was wealthy. He wanted to see who Jesus was, but being a short man he could not, because of the crowd. So he ran ahead and climbed a sycamore-fig tree to see him, since Jesus was coming that way.

When Jesus reached the spot, he looked up and said to him, 'Zacchaeus, come down immediately. I must stay at your house today.' So he came down at once and welcomed him gladly.

All the people saw this and began to mutter, 'He has gone to be the guest of a "sinner".'

But Zacchaeus stood up and said to the Lord, 'Look, Lord! Here and now I give half of my possessions to the poor, and if I have cheated anybody out of anything, I will pay back four times the amount.'

Jesus said to him, 'Today salvation has come to this house, because this man, too, is a son of Abraham. For the Son of Man came to seek and to save what was lost.' Luke 19:1-10

Stephen realises that he is a known man. That despite his years of loneliness and his icy agnosticism, he is **known and loved by God**. He is lost and being sought. He becomes a melted man. Faith springs up where there had been nothing, and his eyes prick with the release of new tears. He confesses Jesus as his new king and is soon baptised. This timid, distant man gains new strength and character through this new faith.

After a brief courtship, they marry. Stephen is swept off his feet by a storm in the shape of a woman. Sandy is calmed by his soothing manner.

But it's not easy. Two very different individuals. They have to work hard to learn how to be a family.

Sandy and Stephen. Two opposites, sharing their lives together, both with significant needs. Sandy is learning that her desire for love, attention and fellowship cannot be met solely by her partner. Stephen's tendency towards self-absorption and withdrawal has been blown out of the water by the emotional dynamo he has married.

Both believe that God has brought them together and their love for each other is deep. But they also have to wrestle with the past. They, like all of us, nurse the wounds of their different histories:

alienation

divorce

abuse

money worries

dislocation

Tough. Yet remember this. They're getting there.

# chapter 11: fallen angels

> By faith Enoch was taken from this life, so that he did not experience death; he could not be found, because God had taken him away. For before he was taken, he was commended as one who pleased God. And without faith it is impossible to please God, because anyone who comes to him must believe that he exists and that he rewards those who earnestly seek him.
> **Hebrews 11:5-6**

I've never known an Enoch. The one mentioned in this passage is probably one of the most impressive people found in the Bible and he's one of the most anonymous. He lived for 365 years, fathered several children and didn't die:

> Enoch walked with God; then he was no more, because God took him away. **Genesis 5:24**

A long and apparently uneventful life merits little newsprint. But, as ever, God's opinion is different. Enoch walked with God and that made all the difference. Confession time. I'm no Enoch, or if I am, I'm walking with a deadening limp. Jacob's limp.

Honesty. Reality. Faith that hangs on in the face of extremity. The stride that keeps going in spite of the limp. I've been preaching it in these sweet tales. Commending it. Now it's my turn.

Sweet tale: My choice, my story of restless doubt.

**I'm in freefall.** I'm the skydiver who realises he hasn't packed his parachute. The tightrope walker who suffers from vertigo.

I'm the pastor who has left his church.

Told by many that I've left the ministry, even lost my faith.

One elderly man even asked me what it was like now that I had lost my status.

I'll tell you what it's like. It's like living a bad night's sleep — restless, inattentive, uncomfortable. That's on a good day. Most of the time I'm struggling against the rewind. Involuntary flashbacks to moments, places, people, barbed with mutilating feelings, ripe with accusation and bitter regret.

You see, it was my choice.

Moral impropriety wasn't my downfall. There was no affair, no simmering sexual scandal. Plenty of opportunity. Plenty of near misses, thank God. Mind you, in some ways it might be easier to bear — the knowledge that leaving was decided by someone else's discipline.

I was popular. Surrounded by people who met God through the sermons I preached and prayers I uttered. Appreciative of the worship style, drawn by the sense of God's dynamic presence. Mostly I enjoyed preaching, sentences fizzing with biblical truths and human experience. On a good day I felt a kind of effervescence as words flowed and splashed from a hidden well. Please believe me — when I stood up in front of the people, **I believed everything I said** and convinced myself of truth every Sunday.

But preaching is also a kind of exorcism. What isn't seen is the previous six days of struggle, doubt and prayer. Usually more doubt than anything else. I'd find myself living with a verse or passage from the Bible which somehow would percolate through the hot rocks of life. Sometimes the verse fared worst. During a good patch I'd make a point of memorising the Scriptures, pacing my study, reciting holy words. I discovered that the Hebrew word for meditation means *to proclaim*, speaking out God's deeds. This helped me. Further study revealed that the maligned Puritans practised the art of self-preaching. This involved speaking out the words of Scripture in order to convince oneself of truth. They understood that, left to ourselves, the sediment of old sin rises and poisons first our minds and then our emotions. Christians were encouraged to meditate on the word of God, gaining a Bible view of themselves and society. As the mind accepted God's ways, the heart also moved into line. I took my cue from Psalms 42 and 43 which see the writer ask himself repeatedly, 'Why am I discouraged? Why am I restless?'

> As a deer gets thirsty for streams of water,
>     I truly am thirsty for you, my God.
> In my heart, I am thirsty for you, the living God.
>     When will I see your face?
> Day and night my tears are my only food,
>     as everyone keeps asking, 'Where is your God?'
>
> Sorrow floods my heart, when I remember
> leading the worshippers to your house.
>     I can still hear them shout their joyful
>         praises.
> Why am I discouraged? Why am I restless?
> I trust you! And I will praise you again
>     because you help me, and you are my God.
> Psalm 42:1-6, CEV

The state of consolation David reaches here wasn't my norm. Years of counselling, leading, persuading began to bite. Without a vision the people perish, so the saying goes. There are times when the people don't want a vision, and then the visionary perishes through utter disappointment. Dreams and strategies mocked me as I realised I'd never see the shapes and patterns I apprehended in prayer and reflection. Some Sundays my forehead would erupt in sweat as I talked about the promised land and the danger of staying at Kadesh Barnea. This place in the desert is a bit like the South Wales town of Port Talbot. On a clear day you can stare across the channel and see the Somerset hills. The people of Israel could see the Canaan milk and honey flow, but they never made it. Neither did I. I wanted to put my life on the line, but it ended up in a tangled net.

Hope deferred made this pastor sick.

In 1994 I enjoyed a curious blessing. Joy. Like many other ministers and churches in Britain at that time, an outbreak of happiness fell on our church and on me. We started meeting several times in the week, eager for more of God's presence. Several people who had drifted away from Christianity turned back to God, touched by this new wave of joy. Others found him for the first time. I remember one mid-week evening, when a group of young people joined us in the church hall. Two of them were Buddhists, the others were atheists. Such was the sense of God's presence among us that they joined in as we prayed for each other. With my own ears I heard Buddhists and atheists praying for each other and others, using the name of Jesus. About the same time, a Christian whose marriage was near shipwreck had a massive turn around. Stirred by God, he confessed sexual sins to his wife and to the church. As a result he started and now leads one of the most significant marriage and relationship organisations in Britain today.

But a year later I was struggling. Two years later and depression had settled. Restless, disillusioned, bored with the work of ministry. I wanted to move, and a few offers came from other churches. My ennui spread eventually to my wife, until the moment of decision came. We decided that we could not face moving to another church. Not for the time being. After nine years, we left our home, church, town, to do something else. Never known such pain. Loving a lovely church and yet needing to leave.

I'm in freefall.

I long to know him fully again. I long to be with his people in the family of faith. Tired of this hobbling, wounded walk. **Why am I so restless?** Why am I so discouraged?

Ministers have numerous initiations with strange names — valedictions, ordinations, inductions. When I stood and recited my vows, I meant every one of them. Preach in season and out of season, visit the sick, do the work of an evangelist. Faith, faithful, keep the faith. For twelve years I served God and the people, holy motivation mixed with more questionable concerns. Like everyone else. Ambition, insecurity, self-expression, keeping ahead of the pack.

It all ran dry. Dried, cracked, vitamin-starved, doubt-scorched riverbeds of the spirit. My sermons seemed to contain more and more of me. They were biblical in content, but the words were driven by my angst. Frustrated with the church. No, that isn't it. Too easy. Caged within my vocation, cloaked in an ecclesiastical cape that no longer fitted. Possibly never did. Must get out, create a more preferable future.

Maybe.

Except that I can't throw out the Bethlehem baby with the bath water. I'm torn between a disaffection with the various forms of full-time Christian ministry and a gut-felt yearning to love Jesus and serve him with the gifts he has given me. Some of those gifts seem to involve preaching, pastoring, leading others to know him more. Impasse. I daren't go back to what I was doing before. Months of depression culminating in a minor breakdown has little appeal. Neither does a life of peripheral, rim-ridden Christianity. The work I'm now doing

I'm tired of this hobbling, wounded walk.

affords professional pride and salutes ambition, but what is that compared to Jesus of Nazareth?

Sloping into church every Sunday, occupying an uncomfortable middle row, I sample an ephemeral paranoia...

'Isn't he the one who used to be a pastor?'

'What's he doing here?'

'Why isn't he more involved in *this* church?'

Why so restless? Why so discouraged? I'm living in the psalms again, that great poetic record of people who make choices and have to live with them. Before God. In particular this one:

Long enough, GOD —
    you've ignored me long enough.
I've looked at the back of your head
    long enough. Long enough
I've carried this ton of trouble,
    lived with a stomach full of pain.
Long enough my arrogant enemies
    have looked down their noses at me.

Take a good look at me, GOD, my GOD;
    I want to look life in the eye,
So no enemy can get the best of me
    or laugh when I fall on my face.

I've thrown myself headlong into your arms—
    I'm celebrating your rescue.
I'm singing at the top of my lungs,
    I'm so full of answered prayers.
Psalm 13, THE MESSAGE

This song tells me that life is full of contradictions and **God's in it all**. A song which harangues God, which is sung to the melody of running sores and the rhythms of agony. But get this. It ends with reckless praise, delighting in a mighty deliverance, completely out of keeping with the rest of the psalm. Here's a man (presumably) with a serious indictment against his Creator. Ignored, overlooked, forgotten. Failing to thrive, and all of it down to a lack of Fatherly concern. Yet it ends with utter abandonment in God's arms. Get it?

I don't. Or, rather, I do if I understand it this way. Here's a poet who understands that much of life is beyond reason or definition and that sometimes feelings dominate. He understands, too, that what matters is this moment. Now. What the New Testament calls the *kairos* time of God. Just in case you're interested, *kairos* is a little Greek word used in the gospels to describe the beginning of Jesus' ministry. It means time, not in the clock or calendar sense, but in the *now* of experience.

That, for me, is what this psalm, and life, is all about. 'God, I don't know what's happening and I don't like it. But **I'm for you**, and I'm going to call on you, whether you're dazzlingly present or strangely hidden.'

This moment is all you've got. Use it.

They shall awake as Jacob did, and say as Jacob said, 'Surely the Lord is in this place, and this is no other but the house of God, and the gate of heaven.' And into that gate they shall enter, and in that house they shall dwell, where there shall be no cloud, nor sun, no darkness, no dazzling, but one equal light, no voice, nor silence, but one equal music, no tears, nor hopes but one equal possession, no foes nor friends, but one equal communion and identity, no ends nor beginnings, but one equal identity. John Donne

If reading *Sweet Tales from the Bitter Edge* has been a good experience for you, look out for Gethin's next book, **Skeletons in the Messiah's Cupboard**.

Available from good Christian bookshops, or on mail order from:

Scripture Union Mail Order
PO Box 5148
Milton Keynes MLO
MK2 2YX
Telephone (01908) 856006

Or visit our website: www.scripture.org.uk